THE ART & CRAFT OF MAKING
CHILDREN'S
FURNITURE

THE ART & CRAFT OF MAKING

CHILDREN'S
FURNITURE

A Practical Guide,
with Step-by-Step
Instructions

CHRIS SIMPSON

RUNNING PRESS
LONDON • PHILADELPHIA

A QUARTO BOOK

Copyright © 1995 Quarto Inc.

First published in the USA in 1995 by

RUNNING PRESS BOOK PUBLISHERS

125 South Twenty-second Street, Philadelphia, Pennsylvania 19103-4399

ISBN 1-56138-536-0

Library of Congress Cataloging-in-Publication Number 94-74319

Designed and produced by

QUARTO INC. THE OLD BREWERY
6 BLUNDELL STREET, LONDON N7 9BH

SENIOR EDITOR	MARIA MORGAN
SENIOR ART EDITOR	MARK STEVENS
DESIGNER	STEVE McCURDY
ILLUSTRATORS	DAVE KEMP, CHRIS ORR
CONSULTANT	BOB FLEXNER
ART DIRECTOR	MOIRA CLINCH
EDITORIAL DIRECTOR	MARK DARTFORD

Typeset by Central Southern Typesetters, Kent
Manufactured in Hong Kong by Regent Publishing Services Ltd
Printed in China by Leefung-Asco Printers Ltd

Publisher's note:

◆ Contents

How to use this book

The book contains ten projects, each having a picture of the piece of furniture, plans and further information detailing the size, then a list of materials needed, and a series of photographs which describe the making process from start to final decoration. There are also illustrations of alternative decorative treatments. In addition, materials and techniques sections cover general matters relating to most of the projects.

The projects were originated by designers and sometimes made by themselves or sometimes by other craftspeople. This gives a different approach to each project and they vary from fairly simple to quite complex. In addition to the basic design and decoration used in these projects, there is a section that shows how the design may be adapted or customized to give different decorative approaches. This provides a guide so that you can follow our suggestions or make your

The ten projects are presented so that you can work through the book, learning and developing various skills and techniques as you progress through the more complex items.

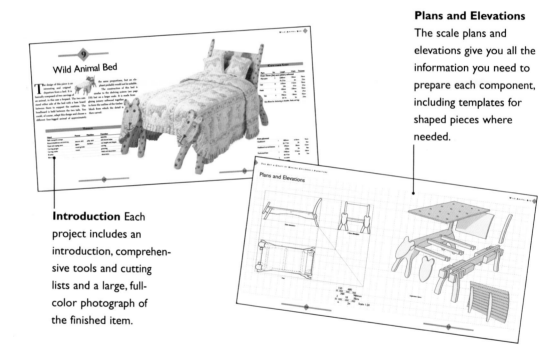

Introduction Each project includes an introduction, comprehensive tools and cutting lists and a large, full-color photograph of the finished item.

Plans and Elevations
The scale plans and elevations give you all the information you need to prepare each component, including templates for shaped pieces where needed.

own adaptations.

If you take the latter route, stimulate your child's imagination and look for interesting subjects. Children may have their own ideas, or you can find inspiration from cartoons, nursery rhymes, and various forms from the natural and man-made world. The choice of subjects is so vast that the only limitation is your imagination. If you do not feel you want to try your own ideas, adapt or adopt our suggestions.

Color is important for children: again the child's own interests may guide you. Generally, children like bright colors, but subtler tones may be appropriate for older children. Mix patterns and textures with color; good examples of this are the clown armoire and the toybox. Where a piece or component is shaped, we have suggested specific shapes, for instance the back and arms of the rocking chair, but some of these could be altered to suit your own ideas.

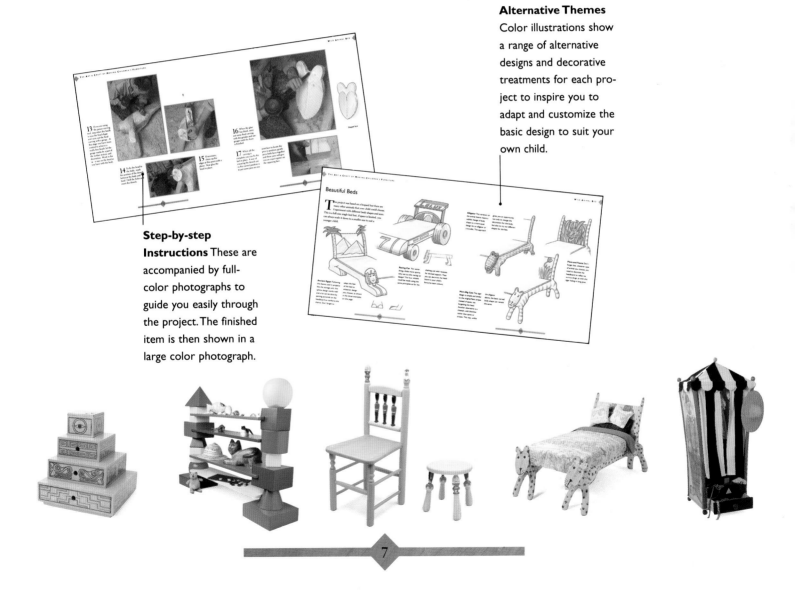

Alternative Themes
Color illustrations show a range of alternative designs and decorative treatments for each project to inspire you to adapt and customize the basic design to suit your own child.

Step-by-step Instructions These are accompanied by full-color photographs to guide you easily through the project. The finished item is then shown in a large color photograph.

Safety

When designing and making children's furniture, it is very important to consider how it will be used and to make it as safe as possible. The projects in this book have been designed for different ages, and of course it is possible, if you are considering any of the pieces for a particular age of child, to adjust the scale to suit.

In general, there are two main areas concerning safety in use. First, try to make sure that a child cannot hurt him or herself on the furniture. For this reason, many sharp edges have been rounded off. The toybox is a good example of quite substantial rounding of the edges in order to avoid cuts or bruises. Most of the pieces in the book apply rounding to a certain extent and, generally, the younger the child, the greater the radius. The second point is stability. Again the furniture is designed to maintain safety in this respect. For example, we recommend that the rockers on the cradle be shaped or provided with stops so that it cannot rock too far.

Another element to consider is the toxicity of paint or other finishes. Fortunately, lead paint is not available now, and most current finishes should not give any problems. When choosing a finish you have not tried before, make sure that it is inert and will be safe when it is applied.

Safety should also be paramount during the actual making of the furniture, so always follow good working practices. Hand tools can be dangerous if not properly used, so follow normal woodworking procedures when using edge tools. Always work tools away from you, and be aware of the position of your hands when holding the work and manipulating the tools.

With hand tools such as chisels, planes, and saws, the sharper you keep them, the safer they are. A blunt tool requires more effort in use, and the resulting overpressure can cause slips and therefore accidents. A sharp tool should cut the wood efficiently and safely, but you should always be aware of what is happening. The same principle of sharpness applies with power and machine tools. It is more dangerous to use tools which are blunt, because their cutting action is impaired and the tendency is to force the material and this is when accidents can happen. Power and machine tools should always be used with the protection provided, although in the book you will see that we have occasionally removed the guards to make the photography clearer. This is, however, not recommended in practice.

Finally, always keep your working area neat. Scraps of wood, dust, etc. can make floor surfaces slippery, and of course the presence of waste can be a fire hazard. It is advisable never to smoke in your workshop, and never undertake machine operations when you are tired or suffering from the effects of alcohol or medication.

Drawings

The photographs at the start of each project show the different designs, so decide on a subject that will suit the child and that you feel happy to make. There are drawings and plans for each project and in some cases, templates for shaped pieces. Basically, drawings are two-dimensional representations of the three-dimensional object and draftsmen use the following conventions: plans, i.e. a view from the top; elevations, which are generally a view from the front or side; sections, where the piece is drawn as if it has been cut through to show hidden detail. These different views are laid out so that each refers to the other and the projections give an effective representation of the object.

The projection shown is called "first angle." Imagine the playhouse suspended in a square corner with a base and two "walls." As you look at each of the three faces imagine them being projected back onto the three surfaces so that the view that you see is represented on those surfaces. If you then cut along one corner and open it flat, there are three views that represent three faces, and they line up with one another. In this illustration the three faces are called front elevation, side (or end) elevation, and plan. Often by drawing only the outsides, not all the necessary information is shown, so make another elevation as if the object had been cut. This is called the section, and in this case the cut is made through the center line. In some cases, it may be more convenient to make this section in a different place; if this is done, the position of the cut needs to be shown, i.e. section through A-A (either complete or a part as shown). The scale of the drawing may be such that more information needs to be shown, so a detail can be drawn to a larger scale. Sometimes it is necessary to show more than three sides, which is possible using the same principle, and all views or elevations relate to one another.

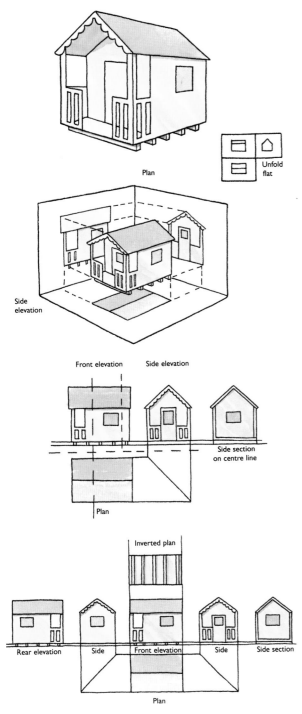

Plan

Unfold flat

Side elevation

Front elevation   Side elevation

Side section on centre line

Plan

Inverted plan

Rear elevation   Side   Front elevation   Side   Side section

Plan

Scale and dimensions

To be useful, any technical drawing must be drawn to scale, and the scale or scales should always be indicated and the actual dimensions shown on the drawing. For most purposes, there are accepted scales in general use, and it is not wise to use "odd" scales. The main accepted scales are full or actual size, larger than full size, or smaller than full size. For instance, full size is 1:1, i.e., 1 foot = 1 foot. Larger scales than the object are used when the object is small and, for clarity, need to be drawn larger than reality. These can be twice full size, 2:1, i.e., 12 inches to 6 inches, or another larger ratio can be chosen if necessary. Scales smaller than the object are used mainly when it is inconvenient or impossible to draw the object full size. Various scales are used: standard 1:4, one-quarter full size or ¼ inch = 1 inch or 3 inches to 1ft, then scales 1:12, 1:24, 1:48, etc; a drawing may have several different items at different scales, so the first thing to look for on any drawing is the scale(s) used.

The projects are also represented in the form of exploded drawings, but the actual details of components or parts of the furniture are shown on scaled grids. This works well, for instance, in the Humpty Dumpty stool, since turning is a very direct technique and generally only overall dimensions are needed. The detailed shape of the turning or other component is shown on a scaled grid which may, for example, be 1:5 with ⅜-inch squares. First draw an enlarged grid full size, i.e., draw each square shown on the page five times the size. Plot the major junctions from the grid in the book onto your full-size grid and draw the shape shown. Sometimes you will need to enlarge the book's drawings to make posterboard or plywood templates as a guide for turning, for laying out the decoration, or for cutting shapes and parts. If you are unhappy with plotting the junctions from the grid, you could photocopy the grid and enlarge it to the required size. Some older photocopiers only enlarge from sheet sizes, but modern machines have a percentage increase.

Laying out from plans

Grids have already been mentioned, but on most of the pieces, laying out should be a simple matter using pencils and rulers. It is normal to use a pencil line for general drawing and a line cut with a knife where you are going to saw.

Materials

Those not conversant with woodwork may not be aware of the woodworker's use of the terms "hardwood" and "softwood." These are not references to whether a wood is hard or soft, but are in fact botanical descriptions. Hardwoods are generally from broad-leaved deciduous trees which often shed their leaves in the winter, and softwoods come from evergreen trees which usually have needles rather than leaves. Balsa is in fact a hardwood, but is very soft, and yew is botanically a softwood, but is quite hard and brittle. Remember this when purchasing your wood.

Many of the projects are designed to use manufactured board rather than solid wood. Many different types are made, but you will probably find the following readily available. Boards made from solid wood include plywoods, where the board is composed of alternate layers of thin wood veneer glued together to form thicknesses ranging from 1/10, 1/8, and 3/10-inch, up to 3/4 inch, and lumbercore plywood, which is made of strips of solid wood with constructional veneer on the outside faces.

The other type of board is particle board, where the wood is reduced to its chips or fibers and then reconstituted into a board material. You will come across this board where you can see the nature of the chips and their cementing resin on the face and on the edges. The other common material is fiberboard, or composition board, Medium Density Fiberboard, commonly known as MDF. The advantage of this over chipboard is that the consistency of the fibers is much more even, and you can achieve as good a finish on the edges as on the faces, whereas with chipboard, you will always have to fill or glue wood strips on the edges. Chipboard is also less satisfactory when screwing into the edges. Few particle boards are good for external use, but plywoods come in several different qualities, some specifically made for outside or marine use. The Playhouse is constructed from this material, the Toybox of interior grade plywood, and many of the other pieces from MDF.

Some of the furniture is made from solid wood, and when using wood, you can highlight the natural colors, patterns, and textures that are available in different woods by applying oil or a clear lacquer finish. Remember it is preferable to use hardwoods in cases where you want the wood to be shown in its natural state. One major problem with solid wood is that when it is used for large surfaces, there is a great deal of movement, particularly across the grain, and a board that was initially flat could warp. This is why most of the case or panel designs in this book use one of the manufactured boards. Solid wood is generally available in planks where the grain runs lengthwise. Because of the structure of the wood's cells, there is very little movement along the grain; the most movement occurs across the grain. When wood is machined into a board or panel, movement along that board or in its thickness is negligible, but along the width, movement can be quite substantial. Depending on how well the lumber was seasoned (wood when felled has a very high moisture content and its moisture has to be removed by drying or kilning), sometimes the moisture content is not reduced to the level where it will be stable in interior environments. Make sure that the wood is supplied to you at the correct moisture content or bring the boards indoors to a heated area so that the wood can "second season" in an environment similar to that where it will be used. The finishing of both these materials is covered in the Finishing and Decoration section.

"Found" materials

Don't neglect unusual sources, for example, if you need something like a cylindrical pole. You could use manufactured dowels or found items such as broom handles. Many lumber yards have specialist sections of moldings. Often these shapes could be useful, from triangular section or quarter-round section for use as moldings, up to the selection of most complex moldings.

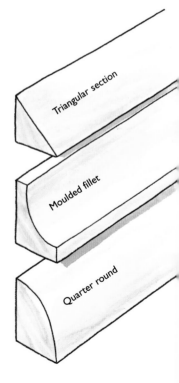

Triangular section

Moulded fillet

Quarter round

Plastics

These are generally quite difficult to use in a home workshop. They are very difficult to glue, and each specific plastic requires a specific glue. Polyethylene is most difficult to join using adhesive and really needs the facility to be able to melt or weld it together. Double-sided tape is often useful for joining plastic, as long as it is reinforced mechanically. In the Playhouse, we advise the use of plexiglass rather than glass as this is safer both during making and when used by children. Some of the projects also need upholstery foam which is not difficult to obtain. The supplier will cut this to size, or it can be cut on a bandsaw. You will also need fabric to make the upholstery covers.

Metals

Other non-wood materials are also used in the projects. There will be times when you wish to use metal nuts and bolts. The Circus Armoire uses special fittings with an internal thread that matches the external thread or bolt. If you want continuous bolts, threaded metal rod is normally available. This is basically a length of threaded rod to which normal nuts can be applied. You will find threaded metal rod in a choice of sizes with corresponding nuts and washers.

Metal studding

Internal thread fitting

Paints

You may use a wide variety of paints or lacquers for decoration, and the only thing you need to remember is that whatever type you decide to use, stick to that and do not change midway since some finishes can react with others and spoil the surface. For instance, lacquer over polyurethane will react quite badly and cause the initial surface to wrinkle. A simple formulation used on many of the pieces is normal house decoration paint such as water-based latex. This is easy to mix, easy to apply, and does not react with any clear lacquer top coat. Artists' acrylic colors are a good choice when painting fine details. They come in a wide choice of colors, but you could mix your own from the basic primary colors and black and white. You can use oil-based decorative paints, but I find latex easier to work with. You can, of course, use industrial paints such as lacquer, acrylics, polyurethanes, and other specialist finishes. However, on the whole, I would keep away from these unless you have wide experience with them. It is also quite feasible to use standard automobile spray paints, available in aerosol cans, and we have used these for the Shelving System. If you decide to use these, make sure that the primer coat and the finish are compatible and that you do not change types of finishes during the finishing process.

Paints Several types of paint are used in the projects, ranging from enamels used in modelmaking, to ordinary car body spray paint (below).

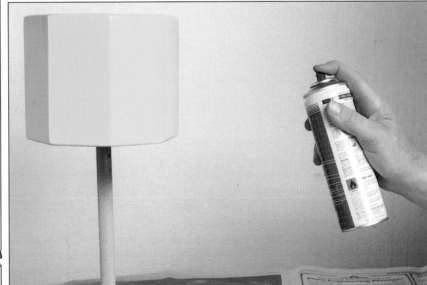

Equipment

You may be a highly skilled woodworker with your own workshop and a wide variety of machines as well as power and hand tools, or you may be a novice with few tools working in a room of your house, or part of the garage, doubling as your workshop. Most of the projects in the book are designed so that they can be made quite simply, even though a few of them were made by designers and furniture makers with an extensive range of equipment. You should, however, be able to achieve very good results by adaptation and using your imagination. The skilled woodworker with all the necessary equipment should not find any of the projects too difficult. The list of tools featured in each project includes machine tools as well as simpler tools, but machinery will help you to work quickly, accurately, and safely. As a woodworker with a smaller workshop, much of your work will be with hand-powered tools and smaller machine tools. You will find that most of the work that we have

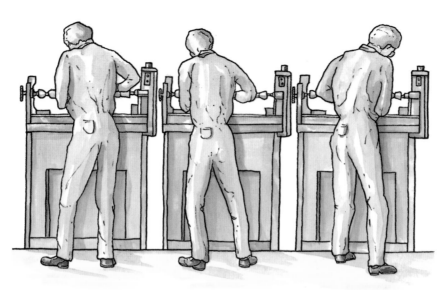

carried out has been achieved using such tools. In general terms, most of the projects need nothing more complex than an electric drill, a saber saw, and possibly a router.

One project that does need a specific machine is the Humpty Dumpty Stool/Chair, and for that you will need a lathe for making the shaped decorative pieces. It is possible to buy fairly simple accessories for an electric drill to be able to turn small details. Initially the wood can be made round by taking square stock, planing along its length first to an octagon and continuing until you have a

cylindrical part. This can then be put in the electric drill lathe for the final turning.

For those with little experience or equipment, most of the projects are still achievable. The first thing is to equip yourself with a place to work; the basis for this should be a heavy and firm table. I assume that the table will normally be used for other activities, so first protect its surface. It is a good idea to cover it with a light cloth, then a plastic dropcloth attached with masking tape. Then cut a piece of plywood or particle board, slightly larger than the table size and

place this on top. One of the most useful things that the equipped workshop will have is a vise, so it will be necessary to develop ways of holding material as you work. C-clamps can be used to hold parts in place. When you are sawing, make sure that the saw line is past the edge of the makeshift top and also that you clear the table underneath when you are drilling. To save time, order your material from the lumber yard already cut to the final size; starting with pieces nearer the final size will save a lot of effort.

Lathe work Work at a comfortable height, moving with the cutting tool and keeping your body balanced (left).

Lift the handle to start cutting

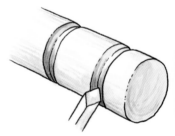

Notch each side of the bead

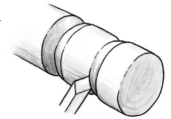

Hold the chisel upright

Techniques

Power and Machine Tools

If you already have machine tools, you will be experienced enough to cope with any of the projects in this book. A good electric drill should be the first tool to start with, but if you are starting off, you can purchase attachments for the electric drill that will convert it into other power woodworking tools. I find the jigsaw and the orbital sander attachments quite useful, and the drill can also provide a basis for a first lathe. The next tool would be a jigsaw, and even though this is generally used to go around curves, it can be very useful simply for cutting up solid wood boards, plywood, and particle board. Third, a router takes over from specialized hand tools such as rabbet or grooving (plow) planes that are no longer readily available. A small router with a selection of bits can accomplish many useful tasks.

When designing these projects, it has generally been the intention to suggest and demonstrate construction and making techniques which are as simple as possible so that they may be carried out by woodworkers who are new to the craft or who have little experience. If you are an advanced woodworker, there is of course no reason why you should not adopt more of a cabinet-making approach, particularly with items such as drawers. Joints are used when parts have to be fitted together, and jigs are made so that the joining system can be carried out effectively.

Planing

Planes are available in several sizes, but for general use, a small jack plane is sufficient. It is essential that you have equipment such as an oilstone to sharpen the blade regularly since the use of plywood and particle board can blunt an edge fairly quickly. If you are not used to planing, take some time to practise and develop your control and adjustment of the tool. In several of the projects, it is necessary to smooth curved work, and here a spokeshave is required. Again, its blade needs to be kept sharp, and you need to spend a little time familiarizing yourself with the tool.

Sharpening

For planes and chisels, the sharpening stone is normally carborundum and needs to be lubricated with light machine oil. You will see that both tools have an angle which is ground and a slightly steeper angle which is honed on the stone. To sharpen, put oil on the stone, and rub the edge to be honed up and down the stone, making sure that you maintain the correct angle and a square edge. You will find that this action causes a small burr to appear on the flat side of the blade. When this has happened, carefully turn the blade over, and with one or two strokes, remove the burr. You should now find that you have a sharp edge.

Sawing

Many of the tool lists refer to a panel saw, and if you have limited equipment, this is a primary requisite since most of the general sawing can be accomplished with this tool. Some of the projects also need some finer sawing, so for general use a small tenon saw is advisable. A panel saw is used for sawing through panel parts and so has no back to interrupt this process. The tenon saw, however, has a metal back, usually brass, which holds the saw blade rigid. Obviously this is meant for cuts which do not go through the material or for sawing thin materials. When sawing curves, there are several saws available; the two I would recommend are the coping saw and the keyhole saw. The coping saw enables you to cut quite tight curves, but the depth of the throat of the saw limits the distance away from the edge to which you can cut. The keyhole saw is designed for working away from the edge, but can only cut gentle curves. Both these saws need an initial hole drilled in the material to put the blade through before cutting. You will find, however, that sawing thick material will be a slow job.

Chiseling

The craftsman will have a wide variety of chisels, but you should be able to manage with three – a narrow one about 1/4 inch; a medium one about 1/2 inch or 5/8 inch; and a wider one about 3/4–1 inch. Again, practice producing a sharp edge on the tool.

Drilling

Most of the projects need drilling in some form, either for insertion of screws, drilling for dowels, or drilling larger circular parts like those used in the Rocking Chair and the Humpty Dumpty Chair. If you have no machine tools, a hand drill is fine for the smaller holes, but for larger ones you really need a brace and set of bits. If you are using power or machine tools, a wide range of twist-drill bits from 1/16 inch to 1/2 inch and over are available. For woodwork I normally prefer the larger ones to have a center spur. Note when inserting screws: always drill pilot holes – a larger one for the shank and a smaller one for the screw thread itself. You will also need a countersink so you can hide the head of the screw.

In many of the projects, you will need to drill holes that do not go right through the material, so it is necessary to make some form of depth stop. On the illustration of the little Rocking Chair you will see the idea of putting some masking tape around the drill at the required depth. This is an effective method, but when you are drilling a lot of holes, it is easy to damage the tape, so you need to check it frequently. Attachments for drills are available, but you can easily make a depth stop yourself by taking a piece of dowel, drilling it through the center, and cutting it to a length so that one end rests against the chuck, leaving the required projection of the drill bit that corresponds to the depth of the hole required. Simple drilling jigs are also used when drilling at angles.

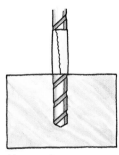

Using masking tape as a depth stop

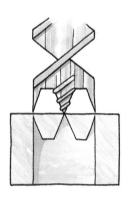

Drilling through from both sides

Hold dowels in a v-shaped block when drilling

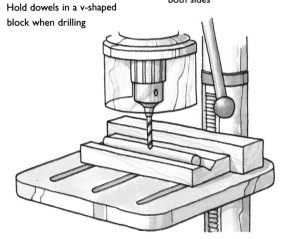

Joints

Having prepared these materials for assembly, we need to determine how we will approach jointing.

Many of the projects use glue and screws; some of them use methods that will be familiar to the competent woodworker. Alternative jointing systems can be quite simple, but of course, woodworkers like to keep up with technology. The Circus Armoire shows the use of the biscuit jointer, where a special circular saw makes slots into which specially made "biscuits" are inserted. These make very strong joints in cabinet construction, since not only do the biscuits fit snugly in the groove, but they swell slightly when glue is applied. However, if you do not have the equipment for this, don't worry; there are two other, simpler ways available. If you have a router, you can make grooves into which you can fit tongues. Tongues are normally cut from plywood, so if you use a thickness of 1/8 inch with a 1/8-inch router bit, you have a very effective tongue and groove jointing method. If you don't have a router, the traditional method of using dowels is simple and effective. Lay out the centers of the dowels on one part, select your dowel size and appropriate drill bit, then drill the holes. Now use dowel centers (it is worth investing in a set of these) to transfer the position of these holes. Put these into the holes you have already drilled, line up the other part of the joint by pressing or lightly clamping the joint together, and the dowel center will be marked on the other face. Drill the matching holes. This method should guarantee accurate jointing. Other joints used include mortise, lap joints and rabbet joints.

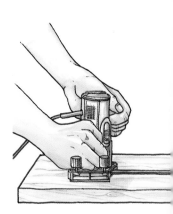

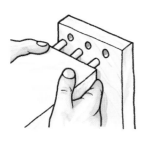

Dowel joint

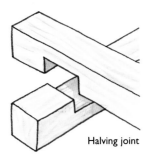

Halving joint

Routing grooves Plunge the router to the maximum depth, move smoothly to the end of the groove, switch off, and then lift the router off the work.

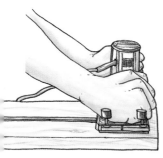

Mechanical fixings

We have made much use of screws, either with glue for assembly, or to attach hardware. Screws can now be found with many different threads and heads. The main heads you will come across will be either countersunk or roundhead, the former being used where you wish the screw to be level with the surface. Screwdrivers have two common driving heads – the traditional slot and the star-shaped or Phillips type. Three types of screw thread are generally available: the traditional screw with one-third shank and two-thirds thread; screws where the thread runs the whole length of the screw, and special screws for screwing into manufactured board. Some of the pieces use nails or brads and, as with screws, there are many different types and sizes. In addition to these "connection" devices, the projects use other common hardware, including hinges and castors.

Adhesives

All of the projects specify the use of a glue or adhesive, but there are various types used in woodworking. You will come across the following glues available under many different trade names. White (PVA) glue has a white creamy texture and spreads easily; it is ideal for internal work and has been used in most of the projects in this book. There are many different formulations, so you should easily find one to suit your purposes. Another glue commonly available to furniture makers is UF (Urea Formaldehyde). In small quantities it comes as a powder which you have to mix with water to the correct consistency and is useful where some degree of moisture resistance is necessary. It is essential to get the mixing consistency correct or the glue's effective bonding will be reduced. There are some two-part UF glues which consist of a resin and a hardener, sometimes a powder and a liquid or sometimes two liquids.

These and other specialized resins, however, will be more difficult to find than white glue and powder UFs, since many of the adhesives used in the furniture industry are not generally available. You may need to consider epoxies, which are used to join metal and other materials, and also to use contact cements. These are normally rubber based, they are spread on both surfaces to be joined, and after a short period of drying are brought together to make a firm joint. These adhesives have been used on some of the items with upholstery.

Clamping

Clamps are either used to hold work or to help assembly and the most useful type is the C-clamp, which suits both purposes. You will need at least half a dozen of these, and some of them should be the one-handed type which are more for holding than assembly. Bar clamps are also necessary for most of the work small ones, $2\frac{1}{2}$ feet, will suffice, but I would advise 3 or 4.

Clamping Use bar clamps to hold glued sections, checking that frames are square with a try square and ruler for the diagonals.

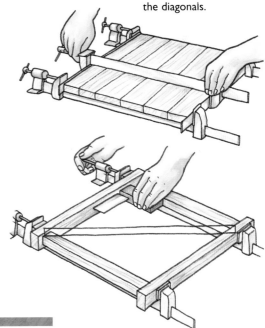

Finishing and Decoration

Prior to final decoration, all surfaces need to be cleaned and then sealed. First clean with sandpaper; at this stage it is a good idea to use garnet paper which is available in many grades, from coarse to very fine. When using plywood or particle board, you should only need to sand the pieces lightly with a medium to fine-grade paper, but you may also have to fill edges or recess screw holes and nail holes, so you may need a coarser grit paper to get these flat.

Abrasives

When we think of abrasives as used in woodwork, the usual term used is "sandpaper." Sandpapers, however, do not use sand as a grit, but other minerals. Garnet paper is the material most often used by cabinet makers. Aluminum oxide paper is often used with power tools. Silicon carbide paper is used by metal workers as "wet and dry" paper, but furniture makers use a self-lubricating "no-load" type. Used dry, it is ideal

for rubbing a finish. Steel wool can be used in its fine grades for final finishing. Sandpapers come in several grits, which are expressed by the coarseness of the grit, ranging from 50, which is the coarsest, up to 600, which is the finest.

You should not try to achieve a final finish by using sandpaper instead of a plane or spokeshave. However, when solid wood surfaces have been smoothed, to get a good finish you need to use a fairly coarse paper first and work up through the grits. Generally, when working on flat surfaces, use a cork block to prevent the sandpaper from causing ridges, surfaces have been smoothed, to get a good finish you need to use a fairly coarse paper first and work down through the grades. Generally, when working on flat surfaces, use a cork block to prevent the sandpaper causing ridges.

Sanding Use a sanding block on faces and edges or wrap the sandpaper around a piece of dowel for sanding grooves. Finish with a finer grade.

Decoration

When the surface is ready, decide which decorative techniques you will use. If you have used solid wood and wish to show the natural grain and color, then you will need to apply a clear finish which will both protect the wood and enhance the color and grain. Apply a thin coat of clear finish first, and when it is dry, sand it with sandpaper such as silicon carbide. Use a fine grit which will enable you to produce a very smooth surface. Apply as many coats as you wish, sanding between each coat as described, and finally use some very fine steel wool with a little wax for the final finish. You will find that this will give the wood a satin sheen.

If you are using

natural wood, but wish to enliven it with a color stain, apply the stain before any finish. Always try the stain you wish to use on a scrap of the wood you have used, since it can look different even when used on woods of the same species. You may have to experiment to get the color you require. You can use either water or oil stains, but I would usually recommend a water stain if a finish is being applied over it. The water stain will raise the grain, and you may have to sand lightly again before applying a final coat of finish. It is possible to lacquer manufactured board, but in all the projects in this book, it has been used as a base for decoration. You should have little need to sand the faces, but if using chipboard,

you will need to finish the edges as I mentioned when writing about manufactured board. With man-made board, you will need to apply a primer/sealer finish. This can be achieved by using an ordinary finish or ordinary paint, but there are specially formulated paints available which prime the surface for subsequent coats and fill minor defects. Apply this to the necessary surfaces and when dry lightly sand with a fine sandpaper. You should plan the decoration in stages starting with covering large areas and finishing with the fine details. This procedure is shown well in the Toybox where, after laying out with pencil, the base colors are brushed in.

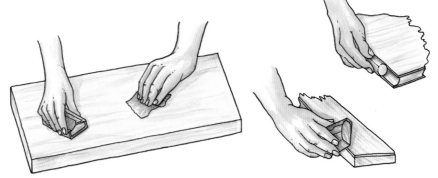

Application

Most of the furniture in the book has used finishes which are applied with a brush, and this is one of the easiest methods of application. You will need a variety of brushes to cover painting in large areas and to paint in the details. Always clean the brushes properly after use. Where you want to achieve a sharp line between two colors, you can use masking tape. This is shown in the Desk project. Make sure that the first surface is dry and hard before putting on the masking tape and, having painted the second color, do not leave it on longer than necessary. You can also use masking tape to paint curves by applying tape and cutting a curved edge with a sharp knife or craft knife.

Final decoration can be painted as shown in the Toybox, but you can also use other techniques. One of the rocking chairs uses "found" illustrations which were glued in position, extra paint applied to complete the

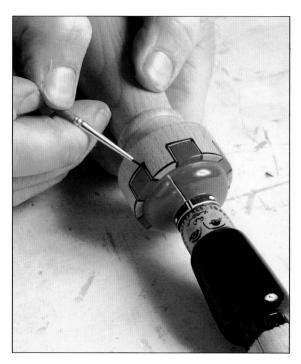

Application Fine detail is painted in enamel for a sharp, vibrant finish (above). The cut-and-paste method (below) is simple but effective, as is sponging (right) to create a textured paint finish.

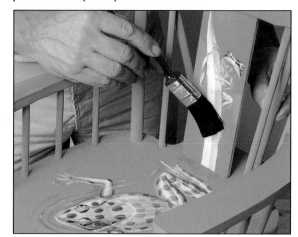

picture, and the whole assembly sealed with clear finish when dry. On the cradle we have used stencils which you can buy ready-printed, or you can make your own. As you will see from the stages in cradle decoration, you need to cut the stencils very carefully, removing only the shapes which will be filled in with paint. Treat the whole stencil with a thin layer of linseed oil; when this has dried, it will stop the posterboard from softening when the paint is applied through the stencil.

On the painted version of the rocking chair, we added surface decoration in the form of found illustrations. If you can find such illustrations and you don't mind cutting them out of books or magazines, you can use them, but make sure that the paper on which the illustration is printed is thick enough that the print on the reverse will not show through when glue is applied and it is set in position. Alternatively, you can copy or trace the illustrations. Another

method is to photocopy them; color photocopiers are becoming more accessible, and illustrations can also be enlarged or reduced.

This describes the decorative treatments we have used in the book, but there may be other effects which you would like to try such as marbling, combing, sponging, spattering, ragging, etc. There are numerous books available which show how to achieve all these different effects.

1

Cozy Rocking Cradle

This is a simple but attractive piece of furniture for your baby's first few months. The construction is very easy, but the result is charming and can be decorated in many different ways. Some components are suited to manufactured board such as plywood, fiberboard, or chipboard; remember that screws as well as glue will be used for assembly and the material needs to accept screws into its edges. Some of the other components will be made from wood, including the base supports, the rockers and the canopy rail.

TOOLS

Hand	Power	Machine	Function
Handsaw	jigsaw	bandsaw	cut out shapes
Plane			smooth straight edges
Spokeshaves/rasps			smooth curved edges
Hand drill	electric drill		drill holes for screws and dowels
Twist drill bits			drill holes for screws and dowels
Screwdriver			insert screws
Small hammer			insert brads
Brushes			apply finish
Stencil brush			apply stencils

CUTTING LIST

Part	No.	Length	Width	Thickness
From plywood or particle board				
Sides	2	26½in	24in	½in
High end	1	27½in	19in	½in
Low end	1	20½in	16½in	½in
Perforated base	1	25in	14¼in	½in
From solid wood				
Base supports – long sides	2	24½in	¾in	¾in
Base supports – short sides	2	12¾in	¾in	¾in
Rockers	2	26in	4in	1in
Canopy rail	1	19in	2⅜in	1in
From hardboard or thin plywood				
Laminate for shaped canopy	3	21½in	10in	⅛in
Wooden spheres	6			

Plus: Glue, screws, nails/brads, sandpaper, filler, masking tape, primer, paints, stencils.

Plans and Elevations

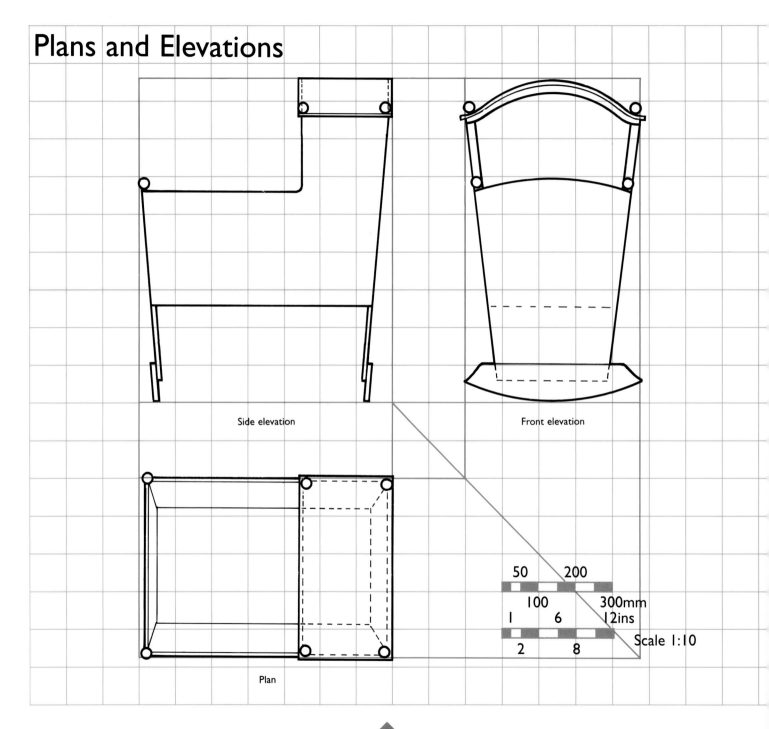

Side elevation

Front elevation

Plan

50	200
100	300mm
1	6	12ins
2	8

Scale 1:10

Templates

These templates are both half size, so scale them up and use the two halves of each template to produce the rockers and the top.

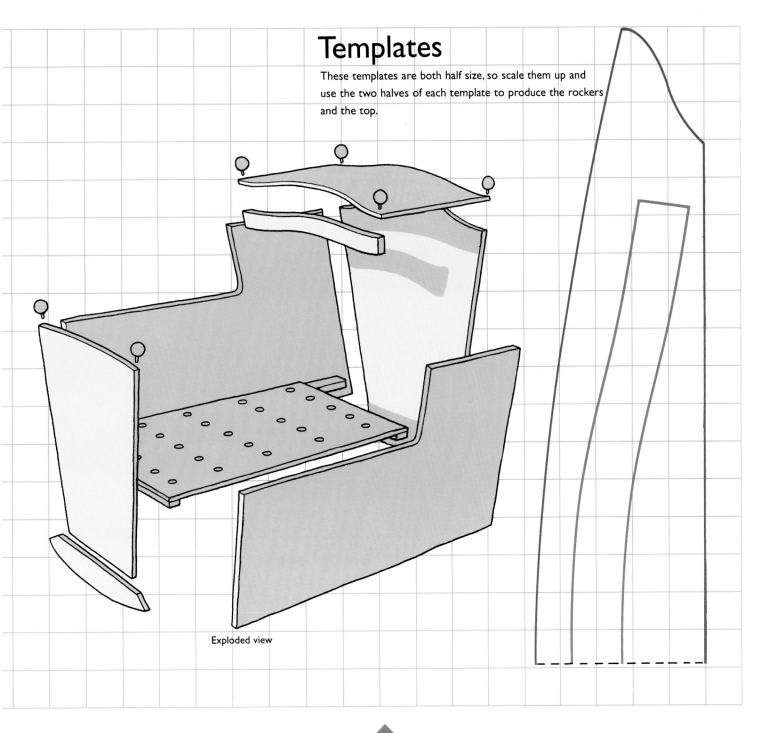

Exploded view

Cutting the shapes

1 Lay out the parts. Cut rectangles before making shapes, curves or tapers, to make it easier to ensure that such shaping is regular around a center line. Lay and cut out the rockers and the bed base supports battens.

2 Start with the two sides (one left- and one right-hand). The low (footboard) end tapers to the base and has a rounded top. The high (headboard) end also tapers and the shaped top forms the canopy. The tapered ends support the bed base and form the rockers. Cut rectangles for the sides and ends, mark a center line in each, and mark and then cut the long tapers. Repeat a similar operation on the sides, cutting tapers and making the low side and high end for the canopy.

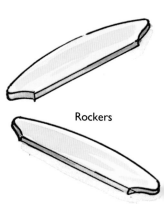

Rockers

3 Now assemble the ends. Mark the position of the rockers and bed base supports, screw the supports in place and then the rockers. The two ends stop short of the actual rocker curves so that the cradle is supported only on the rockers, thus allowing the curve to be altered if required. The general sequence in most cases where a piece is screwed and glued together is: lay out, drill screw pilot hole, countersink when necessary; insert screws dry, check, if satisfactory, remove the screws; apply glue and finally assemble. Next, cut the shaped rail for the front of the canopy; its shape must match the one at the high end.

Assembly

4 To assemble the main structure, position and attach both sides to the vertically tapered edges of the ends. Attach the canopy rail in position using the sequence described earlier. Cut the perforated base to size and put it in place to keep the structure square.

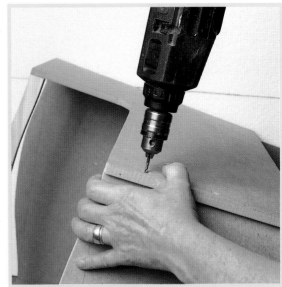

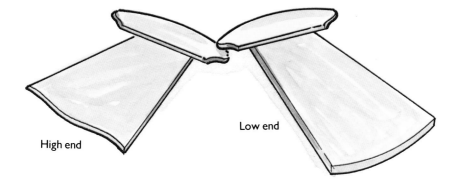

High end

Low end

CROSS REFERENCE	
Drilling	14
Fixings	15

5 This stage shows an interesting technique – that of forming the canopy shape. In industry, shapes such as these would need jigs and presses to accomplish, but for the home woodworker this result can be achieved in the following way. The thickness of the shaped canopy is approximately ⅜ inch. To make it yourself, use three sheets that are ⅛ inch thick and able to bend easily to the required shape, such as hardboard or thin plywood. Spread glue on the top edge of the high end, the top of the canopy rail, and the tops of the two sides.

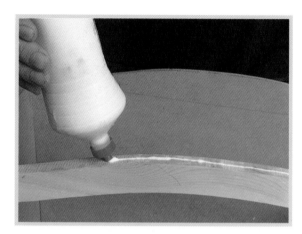

6 Position one of the thin sheets and hold it securely in place. Secure it to the end with brads. You can hold the sheet down to the shape using C-clamps while you secure it in position with brads.

 **Creating curves**

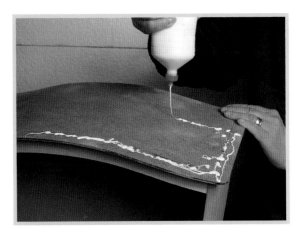

7 When the glue is dry, remove the clamps; the sheet will remain in the shape required. Apply glue to this formed surface and position the next sheet on this glued surface.

Clamp in position and insert more brads to hold it. When the glue is dry, repeat this process with the final thin sheet to give a strong curved canopy.

8 Carefully drill the holes to accept the dowels which are located in the decorative spheres. You should be able to buy wooden spheres or, if you have turning equipment, you can make them yourself. You can use any material to make the spheres, as long as they are drilled to accept the connecting dowels. Alternatively, use ready-made spheres such as door/drawer knobs of the correct size; these often have screws already attached to them.

9 Whichever way you make the spheres, apply glue and tap them into place. Repeat the procedure to secure the spheres at the foot end of the cradle.

Finishing

10 To prepare the cradle for finishing, fill any screw holes, brad holes, or rough edges with wood putty, then sand all the edges with sandpaper as necessary.

11 The cradle is now ready for decorating, but first check the rocking motion. This should not be too extreme as it could be dangerous, so either lessen the curve by planing, or screw small stops to the underside of the rockers at the end to limit the amount of travel.

12 Apply a white primer coat, and when this is dry, apply your chosen color of paint. Paint one color first and, when this is dry, prepare the next color.

13 Before painting the rest of the cradle, paint the decorative spheres. In order not to mark the painted surface, mask off with paper to protect it while painting the spheres. Fold the paper twice, cut off the common corner, and slit one edge; open out the paper and locate it around the base of the sphere.

15 First, cut out the stencil pattern carefully with a scalpel or craft knife, making sure that you use a cutting board underneath to protect table surfaces.

14 Then paint the rest of the cradle in another color – in this case, yellow. When the base coats are dry, the cradle may be decorated with stencils. These are commercially available, although you could make your own.

16 Prepare the thin backing on which the stencil pattern is printed by applying several coats of 50% linseed oil/50% turpentine to stiffen and protect it from the effects of applying paint with a stencil brush, which has very stiff bristles.

 Stenciling

17 Before you apply the stencil to the cradle itself, try a sample on a scrap of board to get used to the process. Then hold the stencil in position on the cradle with masking tape, and stencil the yellow horse to the blue end first.

18 Remove the tape and reposition the stencil on the yellow side to apply a blue horse or one in a color of your choice. Lift the stencil at one end to check your work. When the paint is dry, apply a coat of clear varnish to protect the decoration.

19 Now all that remains is to add the perforated base, a suitable mattress to fit, and some bedding. The finished cradle will be an invaluable part of your child's nursery.

Rock-a-bye Baby

T he original cradle was painted blue and yellow, and then decorated with stenciled horses. Experiment with other colors and decorative finishes as in these examples, try making your own stencils, or use the cut-and-paste method shown for the decorated version of the rocking chair.

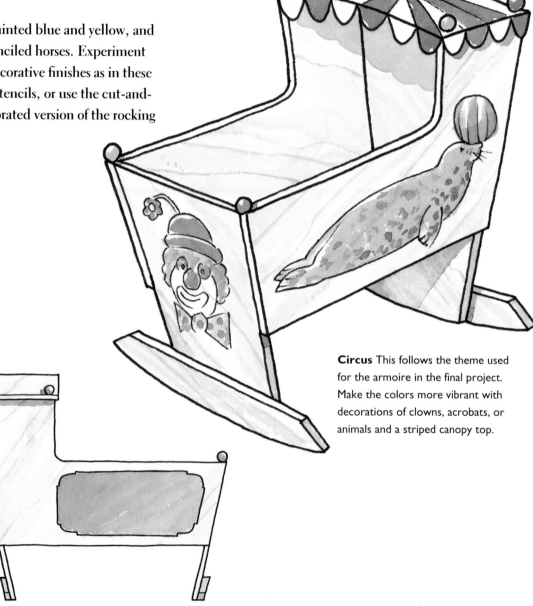

Circus This follows the theme used for the armoire in the final project. Make the colors more vibrant with decorations of clowns, acrobats, or animals and a striped canopy top.

Paneling Another way of achieving interesting effects is to add applied shapes to give a paneled effect. Another view of this is shown on the following page, with the paneling on the high and low ends of the cradle.

Paneling Here we can see another view of the shaped panels continued from the previous page. Try using different sizes and shapes for the panels for maximum effect.

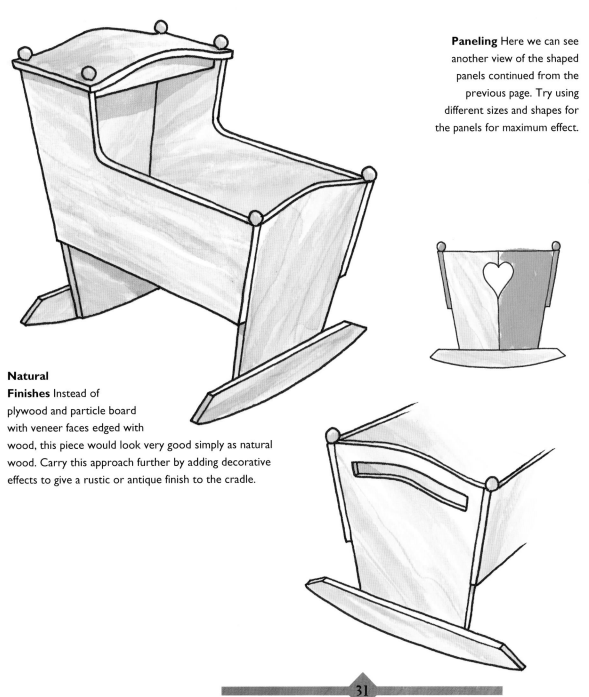

Natural Finishes Instead of plywood and particle board with veneer faces edged with wood, this piece would look very good simply as natural wood. Carry this approach further by adding decorative effects to give a rustic or antique finish to the cradle.

Cutouts and Colors This is another effective decorative approach, and here the heart cutout is contrasted with two colors. Use this idea with simple shapes—circles, squares, or triangles, or with more complex shapes. However, make sure that the structural rigidity of the piece is not compromised by the use of oversized cutouts.

31

2

Desk and Stool Set

This useful little desk incorporates an upholstered stool so that a child can sit and write, paint, or carry out other desk activities. This desk is designed for a young child 4–7 years old, but a full-size one works just as well. The only requirement is to change the dimensions in proportion, remembering that the normal height of a table is between 27½ and 29½ inches. You can see how the parts are arranged on a standard sheet of plywood or particle board, so make sure you purchase enough to cut out all of the parts. Use material of between ⅜ and ½ inch since, even though it can be made with thinner material, the structure is held together by glue and screws and anything thinner than this may be difficult to screw into. Ordinary screws can be used, but it is better to purchase particle board screws which have a double thread and hold better in plywood and particle board.

TOOLS

Hand	Power	Machine	Function
Handsaw	circular saw	table saw	cut main components
Keyhole saw/coping saw	jigsaw	bandsaw	cut curves
Tenon saw	jigsaw	bandsaw	cut joints
Plane			smooth straight edges
Spokeshave			smooth curved edges
Chisel/file/rasps			smooth and fit joints
Hand drill	electric drill		drill and countersink screw holes
Twist-drill and countersink bits			drill and countersink screw holes
Screwdriver			insert screws
Scissors			cut fabric
Needle and thread			sew fabric
Brushes			apply finish

CUTTING LIST

Part	No.	Length	Width	Thickness
From plywood or particle board				
Front	1	24in	17¾in	½in
Top	1	24in	17¾in	½in
Seat support panel	1	19½in	17¾in	½in
Shelves	2	19½in	10in	½in
Seat support crossrail	1	6in	2¾in	½in
Attached seat disk	1	6¼in dia.		
Upholstered seat disk	1	8in dia.		
Foam seat	1	8in dia.		2in
Upholstery edging	1	24in		1½in dia.
(foam insulation)				
Fabric seat cover	1	12in dia.		
Fabric seat edge	1	24in	6in	
Fabric rim	1	31½in	10in	

Plus: Sandpaper and sanding block, screws, glue for wood, contact cement for foam and fabric, primer, paints, masking tape.

Plans and Elevations

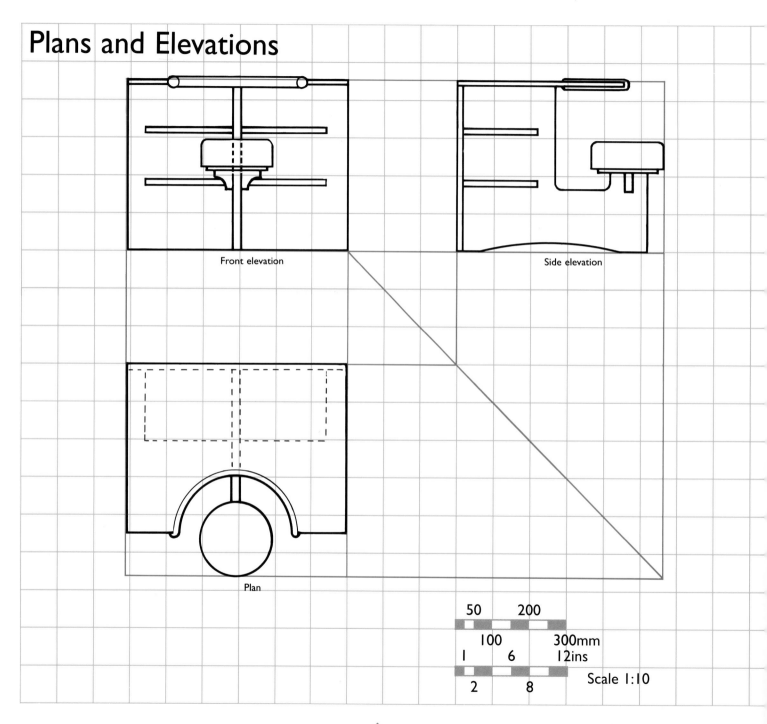

Front elevation

Side elevation

Plan

50   200

100   300mm

1   6   12ins

2   8

Scale 1:10

Templates

This template is for the main support of the desk.

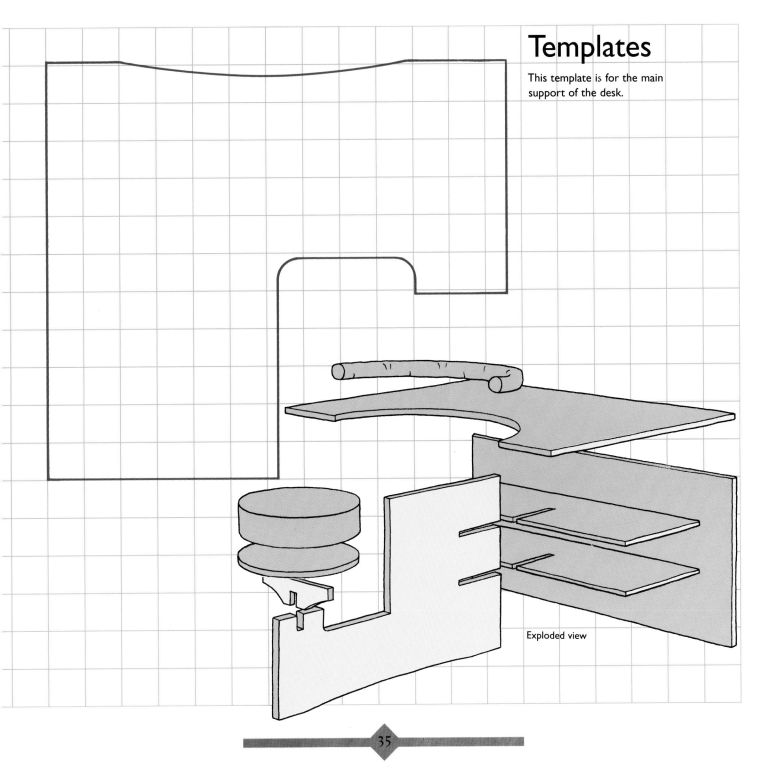

Exploded view

Laying out

Cutting curves

1 First, lay out the parts on the board and cut them out roughly using a hand saw, hand-powered jigsaw, or the combination of a circular saw/radial arm saw and bandsaw.

2 Many pieces require rounded corners; you can use a compass to mark these, but it is often quicker and easier to draw around some form of cylinder such as a cup or jar top. The advantage here is that you can place the object exactly in the corner and draw around it easily.

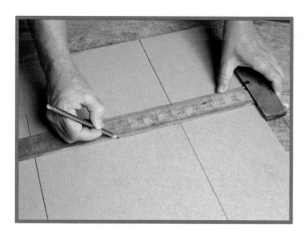

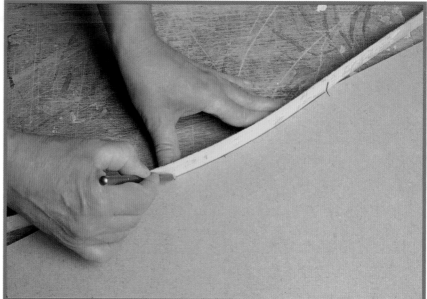

3 To lay out and cut larger curves, make two marks to indicate the ends of the curve and also the depth of the curve from the edge. Locate a brad at each of the end marks. Push a flexible-curve ruler into the curve to the required depth from the edge and draw a pencil line along the ruler to mark the curve.

4 Cut the marked curve with a bandsaw. Alternatively, use a hand-powered jigsaw or a coping saw or keyhole saw.

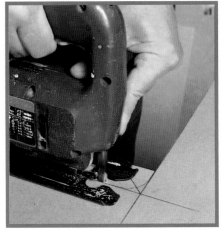

5 The structure is made up of two shelves which are slotted into the upright panel supporting the table top and the seat. Lay out the slots and cut them on a bandsaw by making two parallel cuts. The waste can be removed with a chisel.

6 You may find that the slots need to be adjusted slightly to make a precise fit; this can be done easily by using a rasp.

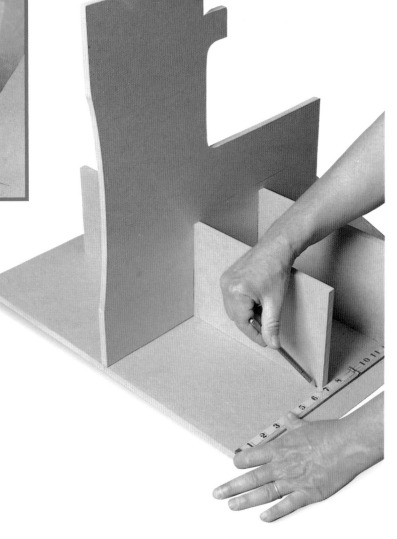

7 When the parts are cut to size, start to assemble the unit. Fit the shelves into the main upright panel, in their slots. Then precisely locate the shelves and the upright onto the front of the desk. Measure to check that they are in exactly the correct position, and mark their correct position.

8 Remove the assembly and mark the position of the screws to join the front to the upright. Drill the holes for the screws from the marked positions on the inside of the front.

10 It is a good idea at this stage to bring the parts together and, when correctly positioned, drill small pilot holes through the face into the edge of the plywood or particle board.

9 When all these holes have been drilled, turn the board over and countersink the holes so that the screw head will be flush with, or below, the finished surface.

Assembly

11 Now assemble part of the work. First, disassemble the shelves from the main upright, glue these joints, and slot them back together. The pilot holes indicate the screw positions. Now bring the face to the assembly and glue and screw the parts together.

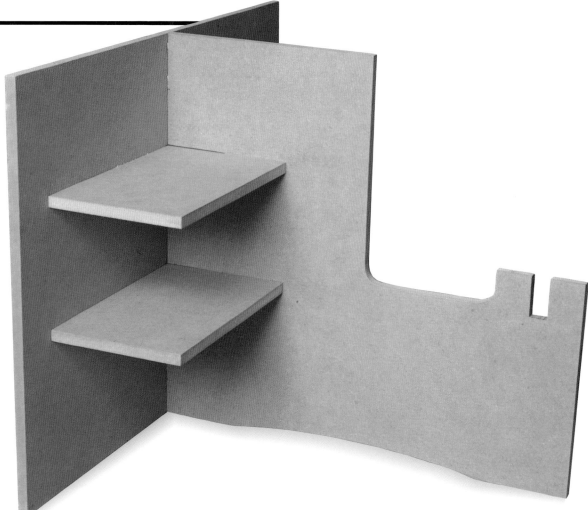

12 At this stage the assembled parts can stand without support.

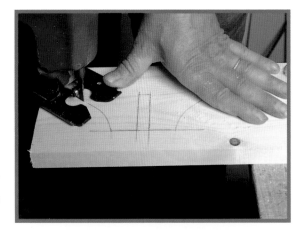

13 So that the seat can be securely attached, make another slot. Make the seat support from a piece of softwood or from a cutoff of the plywood or particle board material.

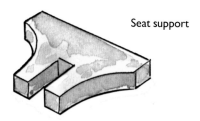

Seat support

14 Cut out the circular seat and also a piece of upholstery foam to fit. Inset the seat support into the slot cut into the upright and place the circular seat in position. Mark where you wish the screws to be and drill the holes. To assemble this part of the piece, spread the glue on the slot joint and attach firmly.

15 Finally, make the table top. Cut this to size, remove the semicircular cutout, then draw and cut out a small curve to remove the sharp corner. Smooth the corner with sandpaper.

17 At this stage, sandpaper the edges to soften any sharp corners. The unit is now ready for finishing. Check that the upholstery foam sits in the correct place.

18 Use a piece of foam pipe insulation as a softening strip and apply this to the inside of the curve. Check that these upholstery components fit. Do not actually apply them with glue until the finishing process has been completed.

16 Repeat the dry assembly with the top, marking the screw holes using the same procedure shown for attaching the front face to the upright and shelves. Fit the top in position to the front top edge and the top of the upright and mark as before from the underside. Drill pilot holes and then turn to the outside face to countersink the screws. Assemble dry and, if satisfied, disassemble, glue, and screw together. When this has been done, attach the seat. Apply glue to the seat support and put in place. Screw the seat disk into place.

CROSS REFERENCE	
Joints	14
Drilling	14
Sanding	16

19 Now the structure is complete, apply the white primer to all the plywood or particle board surfaces. Do not paint the edge of the cutout and the top of the seat, as these will be upholstered.

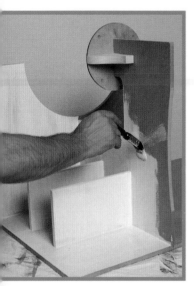

22 When the paint has dried, very carefully remove the masking tape. The edges can now be painted with the bright yellow.

20 When the primer coat is dry, if you are decorating to the candy-stripe design, apply an overall coat of light yellow paint. Allow this to dry, then add the bright blue paint to all horizontal surfaces.

21 To make the candy-stripe design, lay out the position of the stripes and carefully apply masking tape to cover the area you wish to remain yellow. Then paint in the light blue on all the surfaces not masked on the appropriate pieces.

The upholstery

23 Here the fabric has been glued to the upholstery foam; although this works perfectly well, if you can use a sewing machine, the seatcover may be pre-sewn. Spread glue on the disk of upholstery foam and on the disk of plywood or particle board and then glue these two surfaces together.

24 Next, apply some glue to the sides of the foam disk and to the edges of the fabric disk. Now place the fabric disk on top of the foam, pull the fabric down the sides and glue in place.

Using fabrics

25 To make an edge around the seat, first take some fabric, apply glue to the edge, and fold it over to give a crisp edge that will not fray. Apply glue to the top of this strip and to the top edge of the fabric that has been pulled down over the foam disk. When the glue is tacky, apply the strip to the side of the seat.

26 Now turn the seat so that you can put some glue on the base and around the edge of the fabric and pull down, as shown, to make a neat finish. Glue the finished seat in position and leave to dry.

CROSS REFERENCE	
Painting	17
Adhesives	15

27 The upholstery for the cutout in the desk shape is carried out in a similar way. First make a strip, fold the edge as described for the seat, then glue this strip around the edge of the cutout.

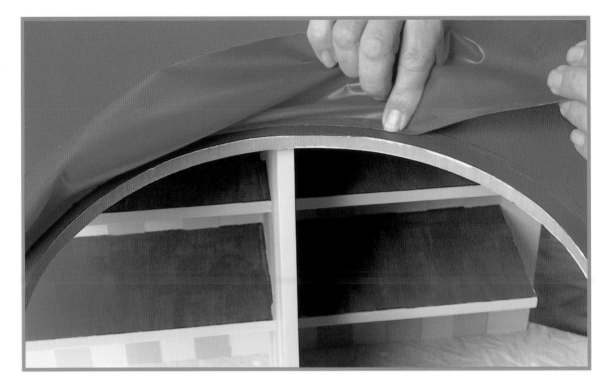

28 Spread glue onto the foam softening strip and position it around the cutout. Pull the fabric over the softening strip and glue it underneath. Make small circular pieces to clean up the end detail here. If you are skilled with needle and thread, the folded edges, which in this example are simply stuck with glue, can be slip-stitched both on the seat and on the softening strip. If you have a staple gun, it could be used to apply the fabric around the edge of the top cutout.

29 The finished desk has plenty of workspace and, with the shelves underneath, is an extremely practical item for children of all ages.

Desk and Stool Sets

The prototype is shown in blue, red, and yellow but there are many different approaches that will give interesting results. Not only can you scale up the size from the original, you can also experiment with different shapes for the top and a wide range of shelf and drawer arrangements. For older children, scale up for use as a computer workstation.

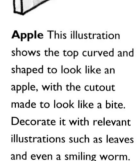

Apple This illustration shows the top curved and shaped to look like an apple, with the cutout made to look like a bite. Decorate it with relevant illustrations such as leaves and even a smiling worm.

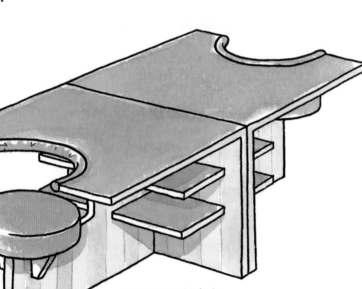

Double Up Homework is much more fun, and a lot easier, when done with a friend, brother, or sister, and this "head-to-head" arrangement is ideal for lightening the load. This could also be the ideal arrangement when playing board games for two or more people, as others could sit around the sides.

Drawing Board Here an extra hinged surface is added to the top to serve as a drawing board for budding designers. Roughen the surface with something like felt, and this arrangement will be just the thing for jigsaw-puzzle enthusiasts.

Drawers and Cupboards Try adding some extra pieces to the shelves underneath to make drawers. Or even change the direction so that they open out to the side. Another option is to add doors to the shelves to make cabinets, as with the armoire project later in the book.

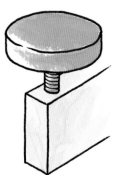

The Natural Look This could be achieved by using MDF, chipboard or plywood that has a wood-veneered surface. The edges can then be filled and painted the same color as the upholstery on the seat and desk rim. For very young children, a rail could be fitted to three sides on the top to stop things from falling off.

Other Approaches Seats can take various forms; here we have a bicycle saddle, and a solid wood seat instead of upholstery. Or try using a large piece of threaded metal for an adjustable seat height, just like in a photo booth.

3

Train Toybox

This design combines simplicity in making with an interesting opening system that also enables it to be used for play. To make the application of hinged parts easy, a method similar to the one on the Playhouse is used. The box is made from ½-inch multi-ply, though other manufactured board could be used, as long as it is thick enough and dense enough to take screws into its edge. If you use large enough castors, the toybox will be fully mobile when open, making playtime even more fun for your children.

			TOOLS
Hand	**Power**	**Machine**	**Function**
Handsaw	circular/jigsaw	table saw	cut main components
Keyhole	jigsaw		cut openings
Plane			smooth straight edges
Spokeshave/rasps	router		work around edges
Hand drill	electric drill		drill and countersink screw holes
Twist-drill and countersink bits			drill and countersink screw holes
Screwdriver			insert screws
Brushes			apply finish

CUTTING LIST

Part	No.	Length	Width	Thickness
From ½-inch plywood				
Top	1	24in	19⅝in	½in
Bottom	1	24in	19⅝in	½in
Long sides	2	24in	15¾in	½in
Short sides	2	18½in	15¾in	½in

Plus: Castors, hinges, glue, screws, masking tape, sandpaper, sanding block, primer, paints.

Plans and Elevations

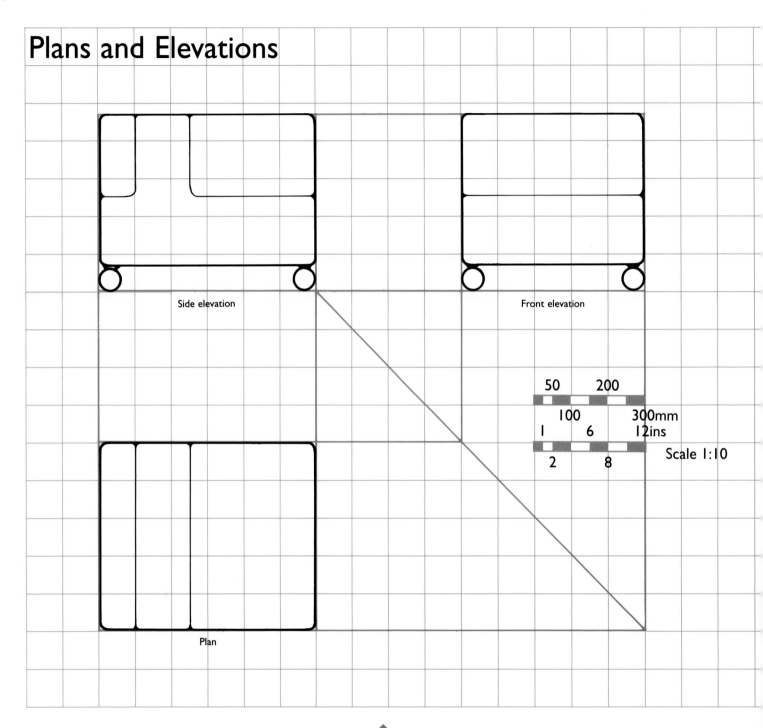

Side elevation

Front elevation

Plan

50   200

100   300mm

1   6   12ins

2   8

Scale 1:10

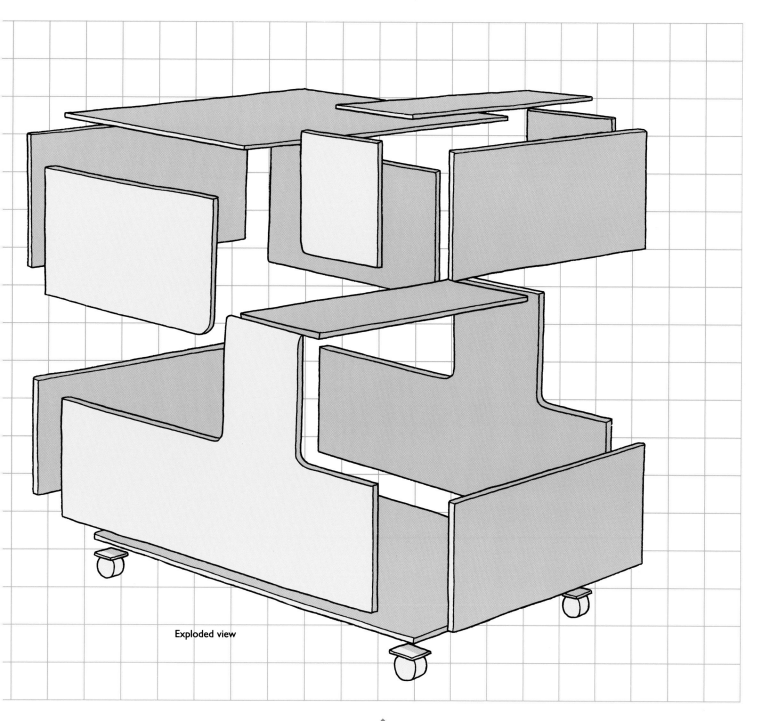

Exploded view

Making the box

1 The drawing shows the parts required. Start by making a simple assembly of a six-sided box that is screwed together and later glued. Cut the six parts to the sizes shown and mark the positions where the screws are to be inserted. These are on the ends of the two long sides, and on all four sides of the top and bottom. Note that there is a particular arrangement of the screw positions around the area where the box will later be cut.

2 Drill all these positions with a twist drill bit that gives clearance for the screw shank, and countersink the holes on the outside faces.

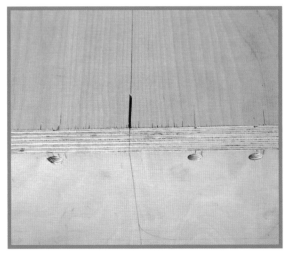

3 Locate the long sides in position on the ends, drill a pilot hole for each screw thread, and screw together. Next, place the top on this open box, drilling a pilot hole for each screw, and screw in place. Repeat this with the bottom of the box. You now have a six-sided rectangular box that is temporarily screwed together.

4 Now lay out in pencil where the lines are to be cut to enable the two parts of the box to open. Disassemble the box and make short sawcuts on the ends where the hinges are to be. These allow the jigsaw to be easily inserted when cutting the openings. Reassemble the box, this time applying glue to the joining surfaces before screwing together. When the glue is dry, you will have a strong box.

5 Make sure that the joined edges are flush with the sides by planing off any slight projection.

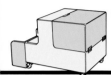

The hinges

6 Now attach the hinges; if you follow this method and sequence you will have no problems with attaching and alignment.

Locate the jigsaw blade in the small cuts in the sides and make a cut across the ends where the hinges will sit.

8 Check the markings for the rest of the cut. A simple way to make curves is to draw around a cylinder. Cut along the lines on the long sides as far as the top surface.

7 Position the hinges with the hinge knuckle directly over the cut, mark the screw holes, and insert two screws per hinge to check alignment. Continue to insert the screws until they are all in place.

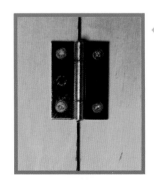

◢ **Fitting hinges**

10 Then cut this slot with the jigsaw. Now complete the final cut across the top, after which the two segments will hinge as shown.

9 Before cutting across the top, it is best to cut the wider slot that forms the handle. With a large drill bit, bore holes at the end of each slot.

11 The illustration shows how the box opens at this stage. The hinged ends will not lie flat with the box ends, but will rest on the floor when the castors are applied.

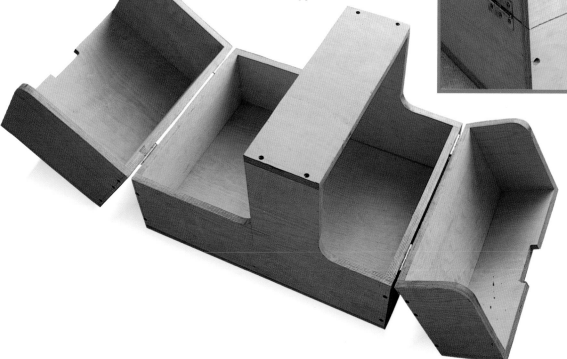

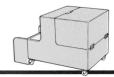

Plugging the holes

12 The main construction is now complete. If you wish to keep the box finish as natural plywood, it is a good idea to hide the heads of the screws by inserting wood plugs. Make sure that the heads of the screws are ¼ inch below the surface. Buy or make a dowel that will fit snugly into the hole in which the screw head sits, and cut this into short lengths that are long enough to allow you to trim them flush later.

13 Apply glue to the holes and tap the dowels into place with a hammer. When the glue is dry, cut off any excess dowel length near the surface. Plane flush with the plywood surface. If you intend to paint the box, the screws can be recessed approximately ⅛ inch and the holes filled with wood putty or

car body filler, then filed or sanded flush.

14 At the moment the box has sharp corners, so soften these by putting a small curve on all edges. Use a router with a special roundover bit on the outside edges, and repeat this operation on the insides of the opening edges.

15 Sand all the flat surfaces with sandpaper to give a good finish. Also sand the edges of the openings and hand slots smooth. Wrap sandpaper around a flat block to sand panels, and around a shaped block to smooth curves and edges.

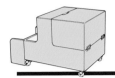

Finishing

16 The box is now ready to receive a finish. If it is to be left natural, apply a clear finish. If you plan to decorate the toybox, you now need to prepare it in the following way.

17 Give the inside of the box a coat of clear finish to keep it clean in use, but paint the outside with a coat of white primer. Apply masking tape to all the edges, just short of the outside rounding – this will ensure a neat edge between the decoration and the inside of the box. Apply the masking tape as shown, making sure that the outside edge is straight. Make sure of a crisp line at the corners by first masking over the corner and then trimming back to the precise line with a knife.

18 Apply primer to all the outside surfaces, making sure that the painting is complete right up to and over the masking tape on the inside edges, and that all the faces are covered.

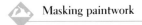
Masking paintwork

19 Now that the box has received its base coat, the illustrative decoration can be drawn on the five outside faces. Using the illustration of the train as an example, measure the position of the main areas of color and sketch these in pencil on the box. You may wish to design other forms of decoration, following the ideas suggested in the design spreads, or use ideas of your own.

CROSS REFERENCE	
Sanding	16
Painting	17

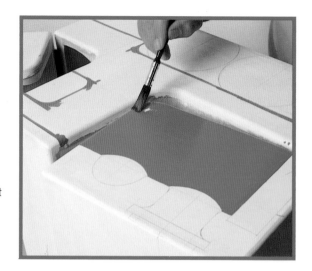

20 When laying out is complete, use a fine brush to paint the outline of the blocks of color. For convenience, paint a straight edge with the help of a ruler. With this outline completed, it is relatively easy to paint in the mass of color.

21 The pencil marks can be finished on all five sides, but it is convenient to paint one side at a time, with this surface flat. Mix up enough color to complete the whole job and then paint each face.

22 Having achieved the overall effect with colors and outline shapes, apply details to each of the parts. The amount of detail can range from leaving the train with just its main colors, or painting close details such as rivets, handrails, name, etc. Paint in this detail carefully on the faces with a fine brush.

23 When you are happy with the result and the paint is dry, apply a coat of clear finish to protect the decorative painting. Attach the castors to the base. When the box is fully open, small castors are lifted off the ground to prevent movement. If you use large castors, the toybox will be fully mobile when open.

Toyboxes to Try

The original project was decorated as a train but this approach is easily adapted to other modes of transport. The castors are, of course, optional and give added mobility to the toybox. Remember to use small castors if you don't want the box to move while open.

Building Blocks The letters of the alphabet or numbers could be used to make the box look like a stack of building blocks, spelling out your child's name when the lid is open.

Ocean Liner Here the train has been turned into a ship on the sea by simply changing the drawings and the details painted on it. Instead of a liner, it could be a luxury yacht or a fishing boat.

Fire Engine
Here again the transportation theme is used, but this time the box has been decorated to look like a fire engine, complete with a ladder and hose.

Alternative Openings
You can also try different proportional arrangements for opening the box, which are easy to achieve. Another variation is to cut the corners and hinge the flaps downward, but this arrangement would not give the same play spaces as the original layout.

Dinosaur All children love dinosaurs, and with this design you can have a friendly dinosaur or a fierce monster or dragon. The only limit is your child's imagination.

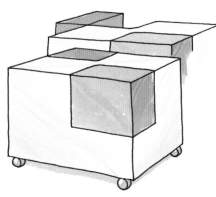

4

Classic Rocking Chair

This little rocking chair owes much to the tradition of chair making on both sides of the Atlantic. Its construction is influenced by the chair "bodgers" who made Windsor chairs in the beech woods of England, while much of the detail comes from the stick or rod chairs of communities such as the Shakers in North America. The design will work well in either a natural wood finish, painted in Shaker colors, or with applied decoration.

You can make the pieces of the chair from wood or from plywood or particle board using wooden dowels or rods for the stick components. If you intend to paint or decorate the chair, you could make all of the pieces, except the top back rail, from manufactured board such as fiberboard, particleboard or plywood. Always use wooden dowels or rods for the sticks.

TOOLS

Hand	Power	Machine	Function
Plane	electric plane	surface planer	plane flat surface
Coping saw	jigsaw	bandsaw	cut shapes
Tenon saw		table saw	cut straight
Spokeshave	belt sander	belt sander	smooth shapes
Brace/wheelbrace	electric drill	drill press	turn drill bits
Augur bits	twist drill bits	spade drill bits	drill large holes
Set of twist-drill bits, $1/32$in to $1/4$in			drill pilot and screw holes
Mortice and paring chisel			cut mortice, chisel ends of dowel
3 bar clamps			assembly
Screwdriver			insert screws
Small hammer			insert brads
Pencil			lay out
Brush			apply finish

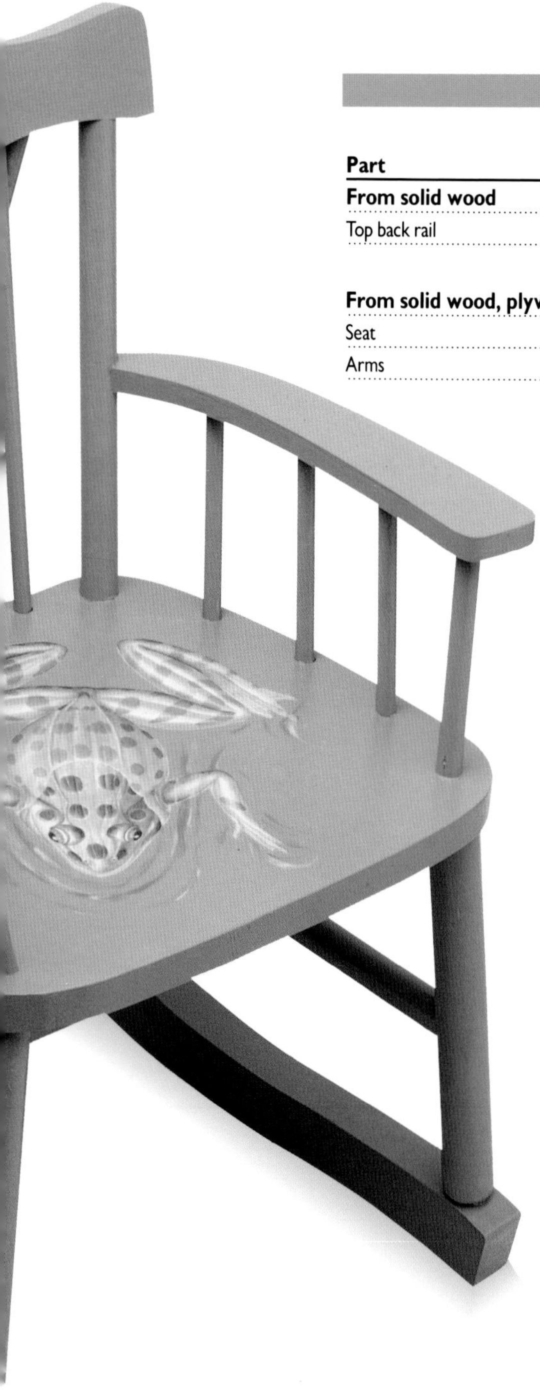

CUTTING LIST

Part	No.	Length	Width	Thickness
From solid wood				
Top back rail	1	13in	2¾in	1½in
From solid wood, plywood or particle board				
Seat	1	14in	12½in	¾in
Arms	2	10½in	2⅜in	¾in

Part	No.	Length	Width	Thickness
Rockers	2	15⅜in	2⅛in	1in
Back slat	1	9¼in	3⅛in	¼in

Dowels	No.	Total length	Shoulder length	Diameter
Front legs	2	9½in	8½in	1in
Back legs	2	9in	8in	1in
V/F back to front rails	2	9⅞in	8½in	6/8in
V/F crossrail	1	11¼in	10½in	⅝in
Back uprights	2	9⅝in	8½in	6/8in
Rear back supports	2	10½in	9in	½in
Back dowels	2	9½in	8½in	⅜in
Front arm supports	2	4¾in	4in	⅝in
Intermediary arm supports	6	4½in	4in	⅜in

Reduce the following dowels to these diameters at their ends.

	Diameter	Length of reduction
Front/back legs	⅝in	⅝in one end, 7/16in the other
V/F back to front rails	½in	⅝in each end
V/F crossrail	½in	½in each end
Back uprights	½in	⅝in one end, 7/16in the other
Front arm	⅜in	7/16in each end

Plus: Glue, sandpaper, sanding block, paper or cardboard for templates, masking tape, screws, primer, paints, varnish, clear lacquer, wood stain.

Plans and Elevations

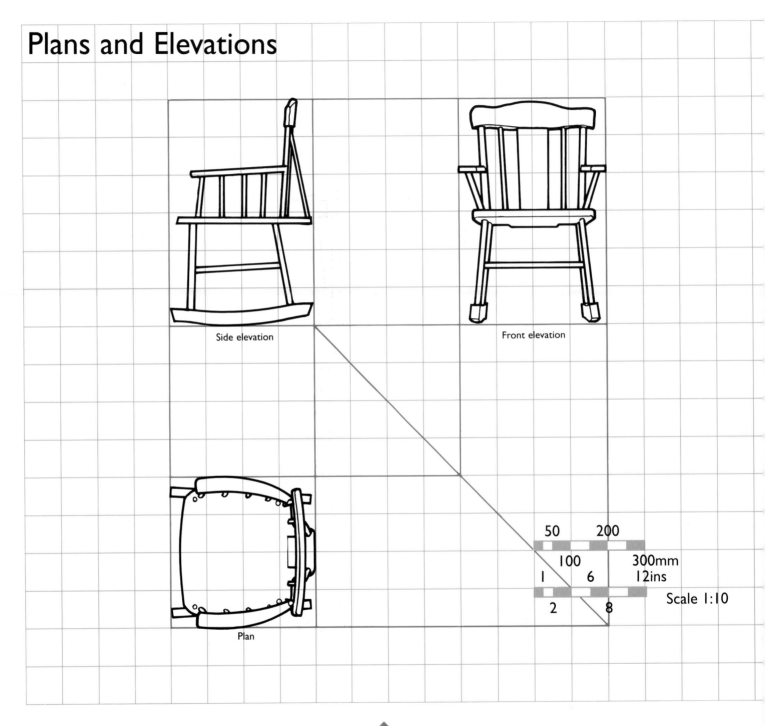

Side elevation

Front elevation

Plan

50	200
100	300mm
1 6	12ins
2 8	Scale 1:10

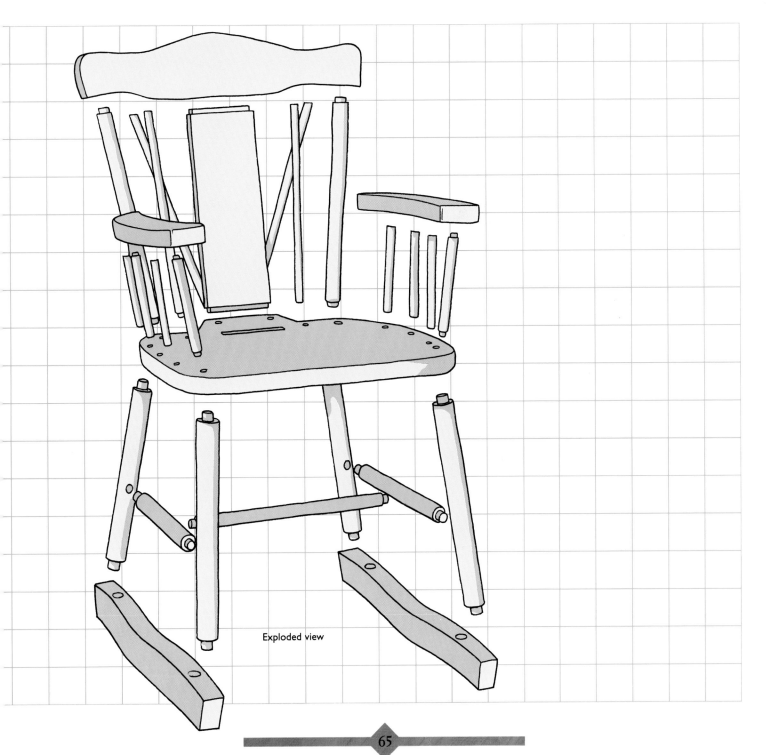

Exploded view

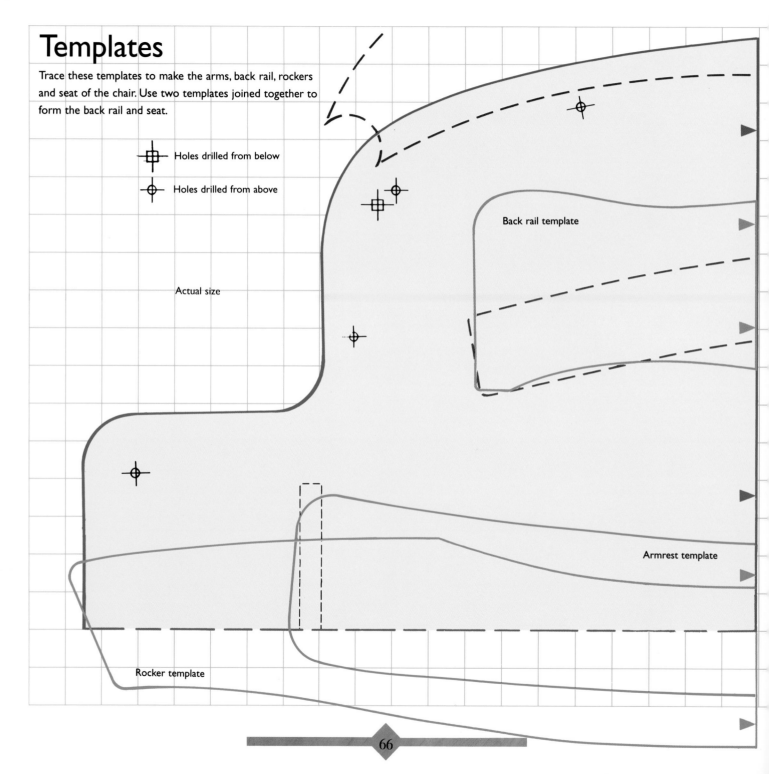

Templates

Trace these templates to make the arms, back rail, rockers and seat of the chair. Use two templates joined together to form the back rail and seat.

☐ Holes drilled from below

⊕ Holes drilled from above

Actual size

Back rail template

Armrest template

Rocker template

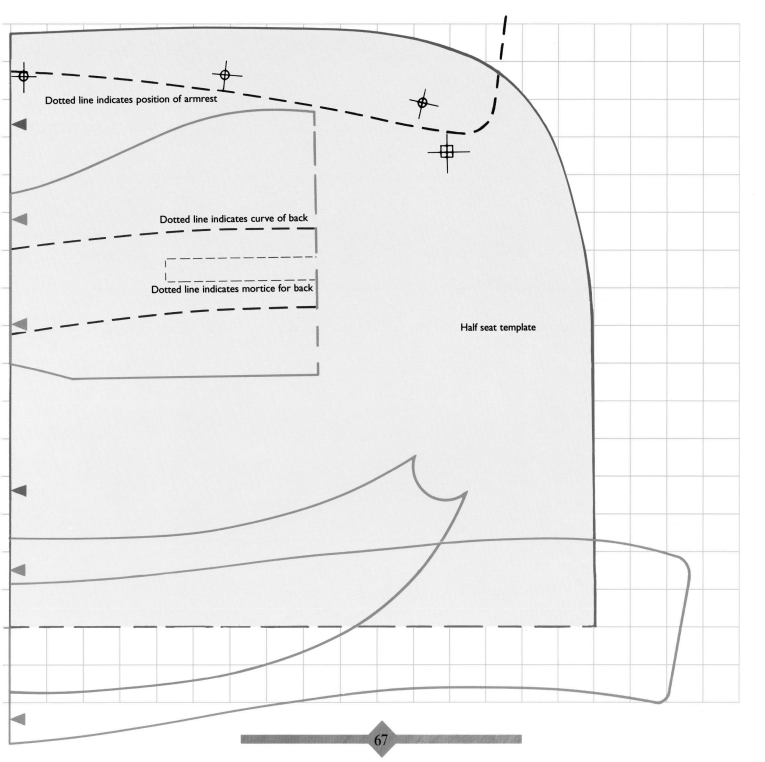

Dotted line indicates position of armrest

Dotted line indicates curve of back

Dotted line indicates mortice for back

Half seat template

Making the seat

1 To make the chair seat, you may have to glue pieces together to obtain the correct width. Plane the edges so they are perfectly true, then glue the edges to be joined and clamp the boards together until the glue is dry. Remove the excess glue when wet with a damp rag, or scrape it off with a chisel blade when partly dry.

2 To lay out the shape of the seat, make a full-size paper template of the seat shape from the scale template provided. Position this onto the board and trace around it with a pencil. Use the template to mark the positions of the holes to be drilled for the dowels. The holes under the seat are to accept the underframe, those on the top surface are for the back and arms. Use masking tape to hold the paper pattern in position on the top surface and use a center punch and a small hammer to mark the center of the holes to be drilled.

3 Cut out the seat to the marked line; if you don't have a bandsaw, use a hand power jigsaw or a hand coping saw. Once the seat is cut to shape, use the template to mark the exact positions of the holes to be drilled on the underside. Smooth the edges with a plane, spokeshave, rasp or file.

 Using templates

4 To remove the sharp edges, you can use a router to put a radius around the seat both top and bottom. Sandpaper the edge.

5 Now drill the holes in the underside of the seat to accept the underframe. It is important to get the correct angle so make a jig that you can line up with the drill to give the correct angle outward and forward. Make jigs for both the front and back legs.

6 Drill the holes for both the back and the arms on the top of the seat in a similar way. Wrap a piece of masking tape around the drill bit as a guide to show that you have drilled to the correct depth.

7 The back slat slots into a mortice. You can cut this by boring a series of holes to remove the bulk of the waste. Then use a mortice chisel to clean out the hole to the required depth. Clamping a piece of straight wood with an angled side along the edge of the mortice helps to guide the chisel and make sure that the angle is correct. Put the seat aside and concentrate on the back.

Making the back

10 When the block has been sawn from both faces, remove the waste by completing the cuts with a coping saw, or carefully on the bandsaw. Shape this cut rail with a spokeshave. A plane can be used on the convex side, or the whole rail may be shaped with a rasp and files. A belt sander is a useful tool for this job if you have one.

8 Cut the top back rail and shape it in two directions from a block of wood. Make a paper pattern to mark the shape on the plan and front. While the block is still square, cut the mortice for the back slat to sit in, in the same way as the mortice in the seat.

9 To shape the block, make cuts through the width of the wood from the top. At this stage do not cut right through to remove the waste, but leave small "fingers" to hold the waste in place, to make the next cut safer and easier. Turn the block on its side and again cut through the thickness; make sure that you leave some of the waste in place to support the rail.

Finished back

11 Next, cut the dowels to the lengths on the cutting list. Some of the dowels will fit into the holes at their original diameter, but some will need to be reduced at their ends to fit into suitably sized holes. To do this, mark the length that will fit into the hole and cut the shoulders on the dowel ends using a hand saw. Using a chisel, carefully pare into the dowel and reduce it to the desired diameter. Work carefully to avoid splitting the dowel.

Reducing dowels

12 When this rough cut is completed, true the end with a chisel. Use sandpaper wrapped around a sanding block to remove the sharp corners.

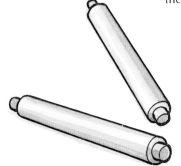

Dowels

CROSS REFERENCE	
Chiseling	13
Sanding	16

 **The arms and rockers**

13 You will need to make two arms and two rockers. Cut these to shape in the same way as the back rail, making a template to lay out the shape first. Lay out and drill the holes in the underside of the arms to accept the dowels that support them.

14 Carefully lay out and drill the holes in the dowels that form the underframe and in the top back rail. Use a drill press, or an electric or hand drill, or brace and bit to drill these holes. Placing a square or sliding bevel on the piece with its blade upright and in line with the drill bit will provide a guide for accurate drilling.

15 Lay out on the rockers the position of the holes to take the legs, drill these holes, checking for depth and the correct angle.

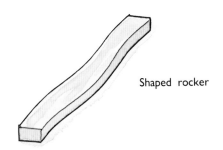

Shaped rocker

16 With all the pieces cut to shape and the holes drilled, sand all the parts with sandpaper before starting to assemble.

CROSS REFERENCE	
Power tools	13
Drilling	14
Sanding	16

Assembly

17 It is a good idea to put the chair together dry, without glue, to make sure the pieces fit, and allow for any adjustment. Try the back slat into the mortice in the seat and into the mortice in the top back rail. Use a chisel to pare the mortice finely to fit if necessary.

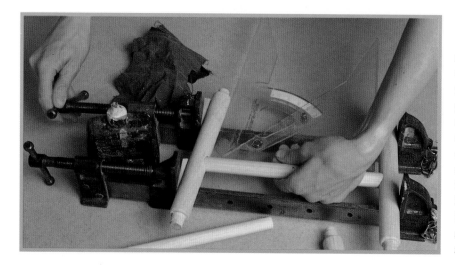

18 Take the four legs and the back-to-front rails of the underframe and secure them together, putting glue into the holes and clamping with bar clamps. Apply glue to each end of the crossrail and insert it to link these two assemblies. Attach the whole underframe into the underside of the seat and allow the glue to set.

19 Next, assemble the back parts: top back rail, the back slat, the main side dowels, the back support dowels, and the infill dowels. Assemble dry first to check that it all fits, then glue the assembly in position at the back of the seat top.

Securing the arms

20 Each arm is supported and secured underneath by four upright dowels. The holes that the dowels fit into were drilled in the seat and underside of the arms earlier. Shape the back end of the arm to fit precisely onto the main back dowel. Use a rasp or a file to make a good fit.

21 Then secure the arm by gluing the upright dowels in position under the arms. Drill a pilot hole from the outside of the back upright dowel into the end of the arm. Screw through this back dowel and into the end of the arm to secure.

22 Finally, try attaching the rockers dry. Then glue and clamp in pl...

Finishing the chair

23 If you wish to decorate the chair with paint, first apply a white primer. When this base coat is dry, you can start to add color and decoration. This chair was painted with a mixture of vinyl latex paint and artist's gouache. Paint the underside of the chair first, then stand it up and paint the legs, seat, back, and arms.

25 For a natural wood finish, use a clear finish. It is a good idea to apply finish, and stain if required, before the final assembly. First make sure that all the pieces fit and check that the finish does not fill the dowel holes or mortices. Put masking tape on the ends of the dowels and on the ends of the back slat so that the finish does not prevent the glue from adhering.

24 Decorations may be painted directly onto the chair or glued on. Select a picture, carefully cut ___d it, and apply glue ___ ___ i ___

Position the picture on the chair and press down thoroughly. When the glue is dry, the decoration may be protected with a coat of clear polyurethane varnish.

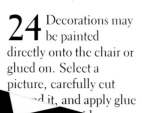

26 Although this is a classic design, it is easily adjusted to suit your child, and the natural and decorated versions look equally striking.

Revolutionary Rocking Chairs

W e have one in natural wood and one painted with the frog theme. This piece lends itself to many interpretations and the following are examples you might find interesting. If you come up with some ideas of your own, so much the better.

The Royal The top back rail has been shaped to look like a crown with two wooden balls as orbs on the top of the back supports. The back slat has been widened and shaped to give a shield with a crest, and the arms modified and thickened on the front to allow the carving of a lion's paw.

Pirate The top back rail has been enlarged to make way for the skull and crossbones and the back slat widened (thus removing the two thinner rails) so that a sail can be painted on this piece. The nautical theme can be continued with rope running between the rail and the rear back support. The larger dowels on the arms can be carved to represent rope, and the rockers can be painted to look like the sea.

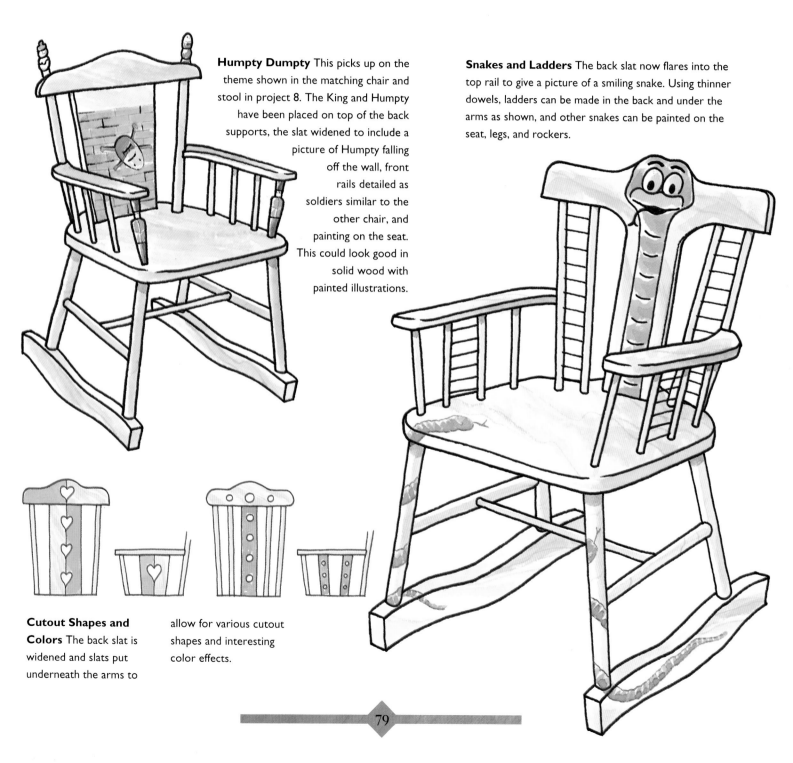

Humpty Dumpty This picks up on the theme shown in the matching chair and stool in project 8. The King and Humpty have been placed on top of the back supports, the slat widened to include a picture of Humpty falling off the wall, front rails detailed as soldiers similar to the other chair, and painting on the seat. This could look good in solid wood with painted illustrations.

Snakes and Ladders The back slat now flares into the top rail to give a picture of a smiling snake. Using thinner dowels, ladders can be made in the back and under the arms as shown, and other snakes can be painted on the seat, legs, and rockers.

Cutout Shapes and Colors The back slat is widened and slats put underneath the arms to allow for various cutout shapes and interesting color effects.

5

Outdoor Playhouse

This sturdy and spacious playhouse is large-scale and is specifically designed for use in the yard. By reducing the scale, younger children could use the playhouse inside the home. This design overcomes the problems of construction and makes the door and window openings simple to make and easy to understand.

All of the parts are cut from standard-sized plywood or particle board, in this case exterior grade plywood, which is used for both its structural and decorative properties. You will see from the drawings how to arrange the cutting of each part: base, four sides, veranda pieces, and roof panels.

TOOLS

Hand	Power	Machine	Function
Panel saw	circular/jigsaw	table saw	cut to size
Keyhole	jigsaw		cut window and door openings
Hand drill	electric drill		drill screw holes
Twist drills			drill screw holes
Screwdriver			insert screws
Hammer			drive nails and brads
Brushes			apply stain and finish

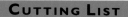

CUTTING LIST

Part	No.	Length	Width	Thickness
From exterior-grade plywood if for outdoors, in 4 x 8ft sheets, ½in thick				
Floor	1			
Long sides	2			
Gable ends	2		See drawings for cutting to final size	
Roof panels	2		See drawings for cutting to final size	
From scraps of gable ends and roof panels				
Porch ends	2			
Capping pieces	2			
From pressure-treated rough sawn wood				
Bearers	9	4ft	6in	2in

Plus: Four hinges, screws, glue, nails, sandpaper, tar paper, or shingles, stain, clear varnish.

Plans and Elevations

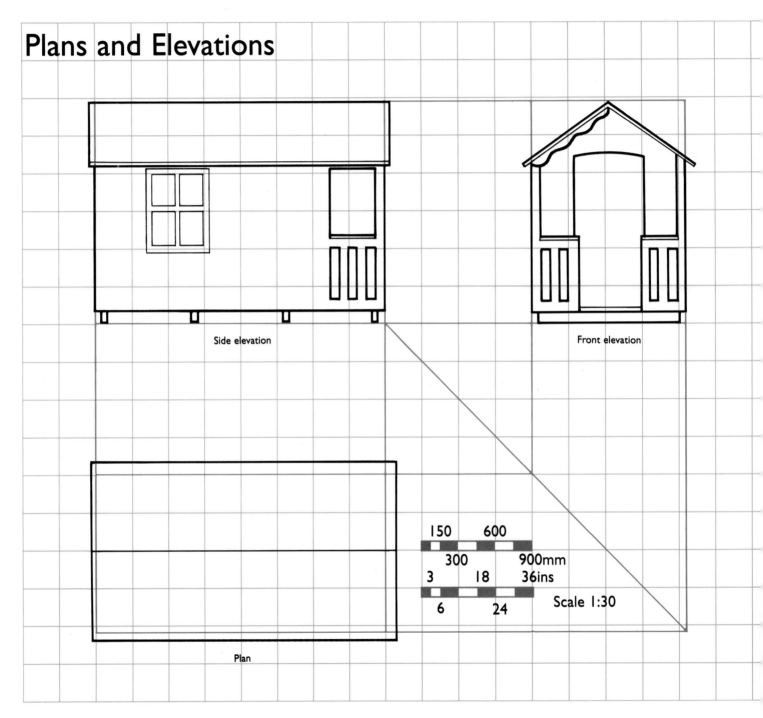

Side elevation

Front elevation

Plan

150	600
300	900mm
3	18	36ins
6	24

Scale 1:30

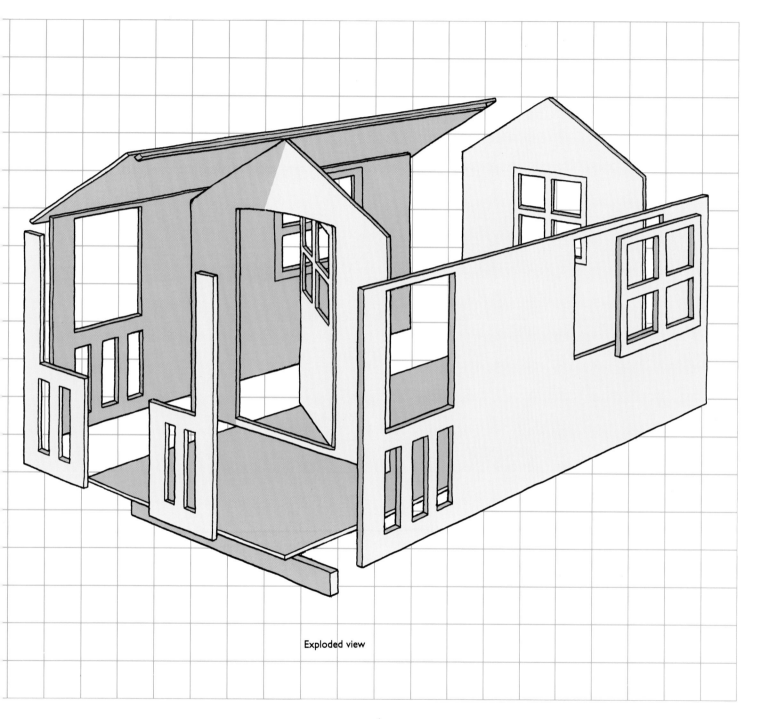

Exploded view

Cutting the shapes

1 Lay out the plywood for the two long and two short sides and follow the illustrations to see how to make the door and window openings. Making doors and windows is normally quite a complex woodworking operation, but this method is very simple and ensures that the openings will fit when finished. The illustrations detail the making of a window frame, but you will use this basic principle to make the door frames too. Start by laying out the position of a window on the plywood. Lay out the window panes and the surrounding frame.

2 Now drill a hole large enough to receive the blade of the jigsaw.

3 Cut out the windows. When you have cut out the required number of windows, prepare to partly cut along the line that will separate the frame and the wall.

4 You will need to drill an angled hole, so make a simple 30° jig to guide the drill.

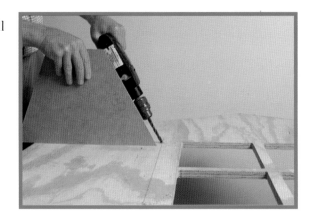

5 Set the jigsaw to an angle of 30° when making the cut. It is essential that you cut only one side of the frame since the principles of construction behind this design depend on securing the hinges in position at this stage. This method ensures that the window or door will fit its opening exactly.

The hinges

6 The next stage is to attach the hinges. Drill a small pilot hole for the screws. It is important to place the hinge carefully on the line that you have cut with the jigsaw, so that the knuckle is over the line and in line with the cut. Only insert a couple of screws to hold the hinge until you are sure that the correct position has been achieved.

7 Screw the two hinges in place over the cut line and then cut the other three sides of the frame with the jigsaw. Make sure that the cut is angled the same way on the three sides as the hinge side, and that the angle is from the outside toward the center of the frame, so that the frame will "sit" into the wall from the outside where it is hinged. When the complete cut has been made all around the window or door, the frame will open easily.

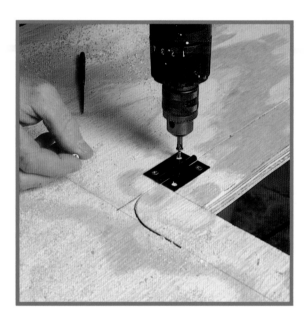

8 A similar procedure is used for the door. Again, make sure to cut the hinged side first and secure the hinges before cutting the other three sides to create the door.

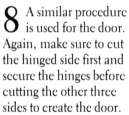

9 In this project the frames were colored. To avoid the risk of accidentally staining adjacent parts, remove the window frame from the wall, noting carefully with letters or numbers which window goes where. Apply the stain, first by brush and then with a cloth.

Glazing the windows

10 This design uses rigid plexiglass to cover the windows. The plastic is safer than glass and is easily attached using woodworking tools. First cut the plexiglass to fit into position. Secure in place with screws, countersink the plexiglass to receive the screw head, and then screw in place. It is better to do this before applying the caulk between the plastic and frame.

12 Now put the plexiglass back in place over the window frame.

11 Remove all the screws and apply caulk to the outside frame and to the decorative trim.

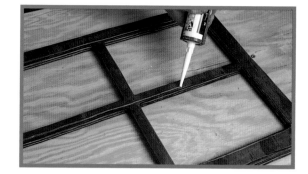

13 Make temporary marks to ensure that the plexiglass is relocated in exactly the same position, edge to edge, as it was when first screwed in place. Replace all the screws, turn the plexiglass over and carefully remove any excess caulk that may have squeezed out.

14 Secure knobs to the windows and doors so they can be opened easily. There is a wide choice of ready-made knobs available.

15 You will also need to cut out the openings as shown on the porch end to create the large, open "windows" of the veranda and the slatted railing effect beneath them. Also cut the topping pieces, stain them to match the windows, and when dry, check for fit.

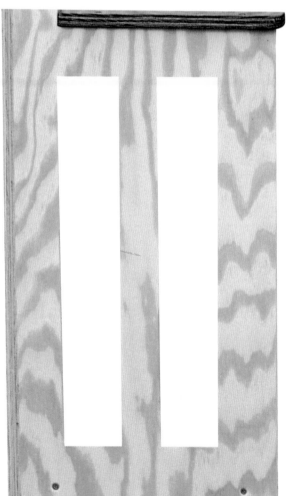

Assembling the house

16 Lay the base in position in the yard. If you used plywood, support it on wooden beams that have been treated against rot. These do not need to be planed; they can be rough sawn wood, and the plywood should be anchored to them with screws. Where you locate the playhouse will depend on the ground conditions, but it is a good idea to make sure that the bearer beams do not sit directly on grass or earth. You can either remove any grass and topsoil and cover the area underneath with gravel, or place the bearer beams on brick or stone slabs with moisture-proof plastic between for longer life.

17 The next step is to attach the rear end and one long side onto the base. Use locating pegs to position these pieces, or screw battens into the corners where the panels meet.

18 Fit the end with the door in position, then position the other long side to complete the sides. Now fit both the front cutout pieces of the veranda in place and secure the capping pieces on top of the railings.

19 Finish the assembly by attaching the two roof panels. Cut out the shaped molding boards and attach the veranda end.

20 Finally, to make the roof waterproof, nail tar paper over the roof and eaves. The house is now ready for its new occupants to take up residence.

21 Add some lawn furniture and perhaps a few home comforts, and your children can play safely and cozily in this great hideaway for hours.

Let's Play House

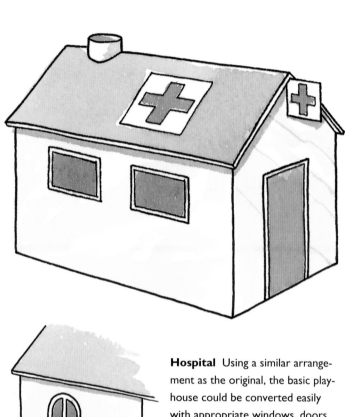

The step-by-step illustrations show a playhouse for use in the back yard, made in natural material with colored stain. However, this design can also be made for indoor use by reducing the scale. When adapting the house to other designs, add the appropriate items of furniture and decoration for authenticity.

Shop or Store With a little more effort, it would be possible to create a shop or stall by opening up one side and having a drop-down counter. You can leave the roof as it is or change its profile. Adapt the door as necessary and then decorate the whole piece with awnings and appropriate signs.

Hospital Using a similar arrangement as the original, the basic playhouse could be converted easily with appropriate windows, doors, and graphics in the form of signs and symbols showing the nature of the building. This way, the building could be anything from a disco to a police station.

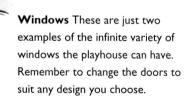

Windows These are just two examples of the infinite variety of windows the playhouse can have. Remember to change the doors to suit any design you choose.

Chimneys You could add a chimney or a skylight to the roof of the house, but remember that this could cause problems outdoors.

Rooftops In addition to a chimney, you can also paint the roof to make it look like different materials such as tiles, slates, or even thatch.

Garage This novel approach is very simple: just change the doors so that they are almost the width of the house and your child has a perfect garage for his or her pedal cars and bicycles.

Added Decorations Why not just simply liven up the original playhouse by adding some flowers, bushes, or even small trees around the veranda area.

6

Aztec Pyramid Storage Unit

This piece of furniture is a different and unusual approach to a child's storage unit since, as well as storing objects, the shape allows a child to climb the structure to look in the "surprise" box on the top. For younger children it would be advisable to provide handles and possibly a support rail. The decoration is based on an Aztec theme, but many different approaches could be considered.

The construction is fairly simple, as the unit is built from a set of similar, but different-sized boxes, each of which contains a drawer. These drawers are placed one on top of the other, but offset to one side and toward the back.

The unit is made from plywood or particle board, and basically consists of the following parts: three "boxes" which hold the drawers: three drawers to fit; one box on top with a hinged lid, and a base to raise the bottom drawer off the floor.

TOOLS

Hand	Power	Machine	Function
Panel saw	circular saw	table saw/	cut to size/make joints
		radial arm saw	
Shoulder and rabbet plane	router		make joints
Plane			smooth edges
Hand drill/wheelbrace	electric drill		drill screw holes
Brace	electric drill	drill press	turn drill bits
Augur or expansion bits for brace or			drill handle holes
spade bits/forstner bits			
Screwdriver			insert screws
Brushes/sponges			apply finish
Marker/felt-tip pen			draw shapes

CUTTING LIST

Part	No.	Length	Width	Thickness
From plywood or particle board				
Drawer holders				
Bottom unit	2			
top/bottom		24in	24in	½in
Sides/back	3	24in	6in	½in
Middle unit	2			
top/bottom		18½in	18½in	½in
Sides/back	3	18½in	6in	½in
Top unit	2			
top/bottom		14in	14in	½in
Sides-back	3	14in	6in	½in
Surprise box sides	4	9in	8in	½in
Base	1	9in	9in	½in
Top, halved diagonally	1	9in	9in	½in
Bottom drawer base	1	22½in	22½in	½in
back/front	2	23in	5in	½in
sides	2	22½in	5in	½in
Middle drawer base	1	17in	17in	½in
back/front	2	17½in	5in	½in
sides	2	17in	5in	½in
Top drawer base	1	12½in	12½in	½in
back/front	2	13in	5in	½in
sides	2	12½in	5in	½in
From solid wood				
Base	4	23in	2in	1¾in

Plus: Piano hinge, glue, screws, filler, nails/brads, sandpaper, primer, paints.

Plans and Elevations

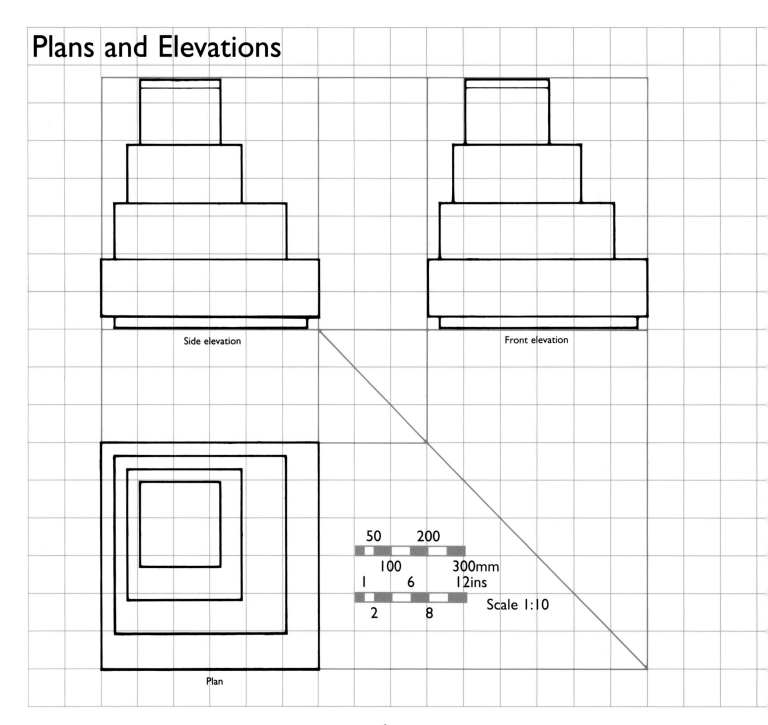

Side elevation

Front elevation

Plan

50	200
100	300mm
1	6	12ins
2	8

Scale 1:10

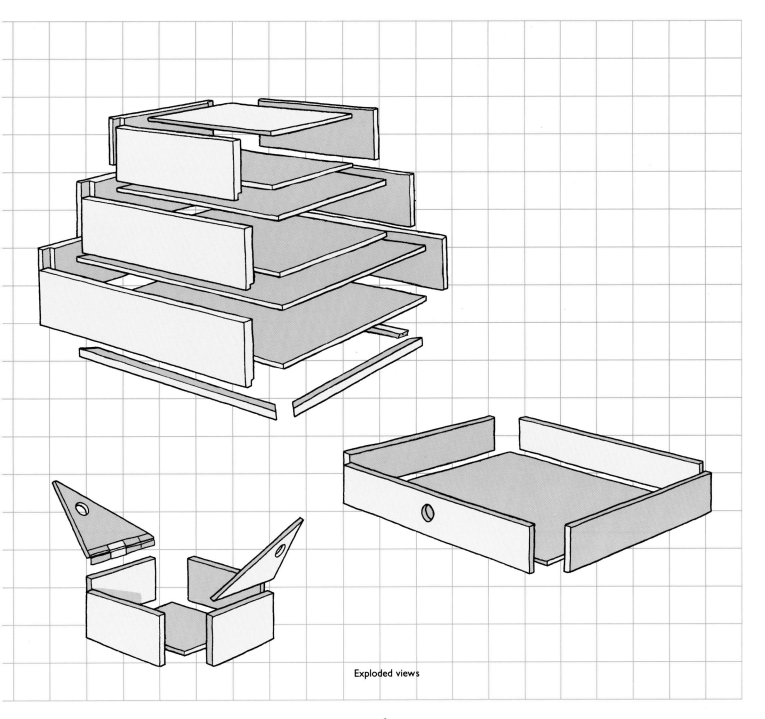

Exploded views

The drawer holders

1 First make the "boxes" or drawer holders. These are all five-sided boxes, square on plan, the open side of which will accept the drawer. They are all made in the same way, differing only in size.

2 Cut the top and bottom of each drawer holder to size. Having cut one corner precisely square, the two parts can be made to the precise size by clamping a stop to the fence and then cutting sides three and four. A radial arm saw is used here but a table saw will do; or they can be cut carefully by hand.

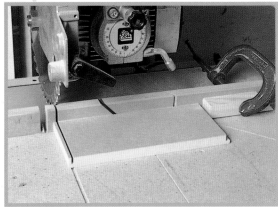

3 Now cut the back and two sides to width and just over length. In order to locate the sides accurately, the back has a rabbet cut worked at the ends. Therefore this will be the same length as the top/ bottom. The sides are slightly shorter to accept this rabbet. Cut the overall lengths using the same stop positions as for the top. Then cut the rabbets on the back parts by inserting a spacer equal to the thickness of the side material.

4 Remember to adjust the depth so that a cut is made halfway through the thickness only. The excess outside the shoulder line can now be removed to the same depth by making several cuts. Now cut the two sides to length. They will be shorter than the top by the thickness of the rabbet.

5 The top and bottom can be prepared ready for assembly. Mark the positions of the screw holes, drill pilot holes to receive the screws, and then countersink these to accept the screw head. To help the drawers run smooth, you can attach some iron-on drawer runner tape along the sides where they meet the bottom.

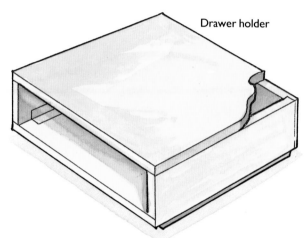

Drawer holder

6 Locate the top on the three sides, having first secured the rabbet on the back corners. It is wise to insert the screws without gluing the joint so that you can check that everything is square. Remember that the front of this box will accept the drawer and the inside space between the two sides needs to be exactly parallel, so cut a scrap piece to a length that is exactly the distance between the rabbet shoulders and place this at the front opening. This will ensure the correct dimension and thus make the sides parallel.

7 Follow the same procedure with the bottom and, if it all fits, remove the screws, apply glue, and reassemble. When the glue is dry, fill all the screw heads and finally shave the box sides with a plane to make them flat and smooth. Repeat the procedure with the other two drawer holders.

The surprise box

8 Now make the "carcass" of the surprise box. It is made in a similar way to the other boxes, but the open face is the top rather than one of the sides. When assembly is complete, hold the box in the vise and smooth the outside surfaces.

9 Before assembling the complete unit, make and attach the top flaps to this box. Cut the two triangles to size and drill a hole in a corner of each to act as handles. Set the marking gauge to the piano hinge, from one edge to the center of the knuckle.

10 Gauge the two sides where you will fit the hinge. Reset the gauge to the thickness of the closed hinge and gauge the thickness.

11 Make a shallow rabbet on these two sides and position the hinge in the rabbet so that the closed hinge is level with the inside surface.

12 Lay the triangular flaps in place, and mark the position of the hinges, and then the position of the screw holes.

13 Now attach the flaps in position and check that they open and close correctly.

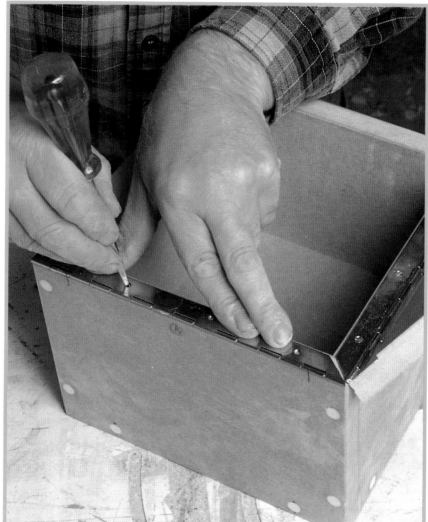

14 Then remove the flaps, true up the closing edge, and apply a sealer coat to that edge. The three drawer boxes and the surprise box are now ready for assembly.

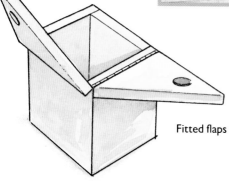

Fitted flaps

Drawer making and assembly

15 Apply the base to the bottom of the lower drawer holder. This is made from four lengths, mitered at the corners and screwed and glued into position, approximately 1¼ inches from the outside edge. Mark the position of the next drawer holder and insert two screws at the open drawer face to hold its position. Do not glue this assembly yet, as it is easier to apply a finish to the separate parts.

16 Continue positioning all the drawer holders and the surprise box.

17 Now make the drawers to fit the drawer holders – prepare a base and four sides. The drawers are made in a similar way to the drawer holders, but the base sits in rabbets in the sides. Use a router to make rabbets so that the sides can be attached to the drawer bottom in a similar way to the drawers of the circus armoire.

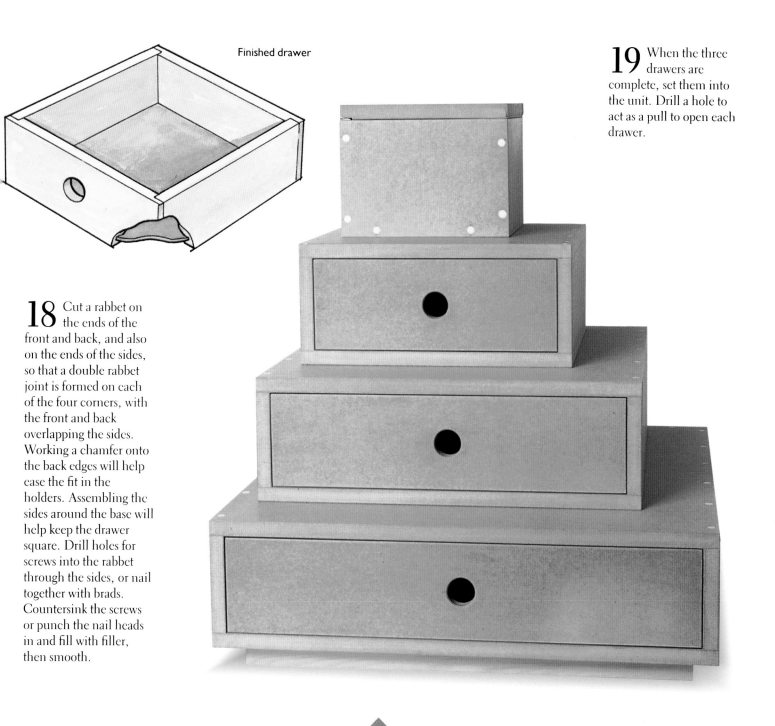

Finished drawer

18 Cut a rabbet on the ends of the front and back, and also on the ends of the sides, so that a double rabbet joint is formed on each of the four corners, with the front and back overlapping the sides. Working a chamfer onto the back edges will help ease the fit in the holders. Assembling the sides around the base will help keep the drawer square. Drill holes for screws into the rabbet through the sides, or nail together with brads. Countersink the screws or punch the nail heads in and fill with filler, then smooth.

19 When the three drawers are complete, set them into the unit. Drill a hole to act as a pull to open each drawer.

Decorating

20 Now disassemble the unit prior to decorating. Mask the top of each drawer holder just inside the position of the one on top. Apply a coat of primer on all parts, including the fronts of the drawers. The final colors and decorative motifs can now be applied.

21 Add texture to the paint surface using a sponge and mix some paint to finish the details.

22 When the textured base coat has dried, apply the decorative motifs. They can be painted on, but here we used permanent markers to draw the patterns. First, mark them using tracing paper to transfer the pattern; the straight lines can be drawn with a ruler.

24 This highly original chest of drawers is very strong and well-made, with plenty of storage space and the added attraction of the "secret" box for your child's special possessions.

23 The curves and other patterns are then drawn by hand. When the decoration is finished, seal the whole piece with clear finish to protect it.

The Storage Depot

As mentioned earlier in the project, this is an extremely strong unit that will easily cope with children climbing on it. For very small children, however, add some handrails at the corners as an extra safety measure. Your children will enjoy painting and decorating the drawers in their own designs.

Native Tent Following the theme of ancient civilizations, create a Native American variation with poles attached to the corners of the drawers and canvas sides added to suggest a tepee or wigwam and decorated with suitable motifs.

Building Blocks Another approach is to paint the cabinets as colored blocks with letters on them, like a tower of building blocks. This design could then be matched to the toybox and the shelving unit shown later in the book. Experiment with the many combinations of letters, numbers, and colors.

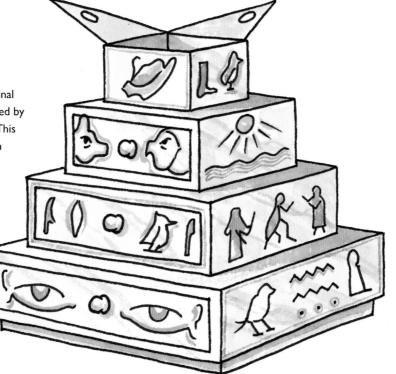

Ancient Egypt Similar to the original Aztec theme, this variation is inspired by Egyptian figures and hieroglyphics. This design is great fun, as your child can create his or her personal rebus puzzle, perhaps leading to the secret of the surprise box at the top—a little like Indiana Jones on his adventures.

Drawer Variants There are, of course, alternative drawer arrangements. If you have enough space, the drawers can be made to open from each of the four sides, with the secret compartment having a lift-off lid and the bottom two drawers split. Having decided on a theme, you could also paint each face the same, as dummy drawers.

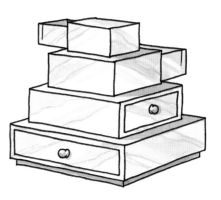

7

Shapely Shelves

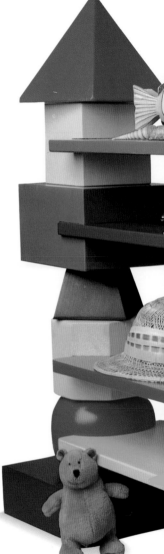

This shelving system is based on a series of geometric solids; the one illustrated was made to suit smaller children. It is possible, however, to increase the size for older children simply by altering the ratio of the measurements. The system is made in component form so you will have to make the support poles/bases, the shelves, and a series of geometric solids: rectangles, cubes, cylinders, pyramids, cones, spheres, etc. The two support poles are made from wooden rods, such as readily available large dowels or broomsticks, while the bases are made from plywood or particle board. The shelves can also be made from plywood or particle board or, as in this example, from solid wood. Make the shapes by gluing together cabinet-grade softwood to sizes large enough from which to cut the required components. This practical system should be as colorful as possible.

TOOLS

Hand	Power	Machine	Function
4 or 6 bar clamps			hold glued blocks
Handsaw	circular/jigsaw	radial arm saw/ table saw	cut softwood to length/make joints
Plane			smooth surfaces
Hand drill and brace	electric drill	drill press	drill for base holes
Auger bits, expansion bit, spade, and forstner bits			drill holes
Brushes			apply finish

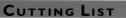

CUTTING LIST

Part	No.	Length	Width	Thickness
From ½ inch plywood or particle board				
Base sides	8	12in	4in	½in
Base tops	2	12in	12in	½in
From wooden rod or dowel				
Support poles	2	35in	1¼in dia.	
From solid wood				
Shelves	4	36½in	8in	1in

Solids

From 24ft x 9in x 2in cabinet-grade softwood.

	Dimensions after shaping	Starting length	Cut into (number of pieces)/length
Top pyramid	8 x 8 x 8in	31½in	(4 pieces)/8in
Top sphere	8½in dia.	31½in	(4)/8in
2 top cubes	6 x 6 x 6in	2 pieces of 17¾in	(3)/6in
Rectangle	10 x 8 x 6in	29½in	(3)/10in
Cylinder	8in dia. x 6in	23½in	(3)/8in
Truncated pyramid	6 x 6 x 4in	12in	(2)/6in
Small cube	4 x 4 x 4in	8in	(2)/4in
Octagon	7 x 7 x 6in	23½in	(3)/8in
Rectangle	8 x 8 x 6in	23½in	(3)/8in
Sphere	6¾in dia. x 6in	21½in	(3)/7in
Cone	8in dia. x 6in	23½in	(3)/8in

Plus: Glue, brads, sandpaper, filler, primer, paints, clear varnish.

Plans and Elevations

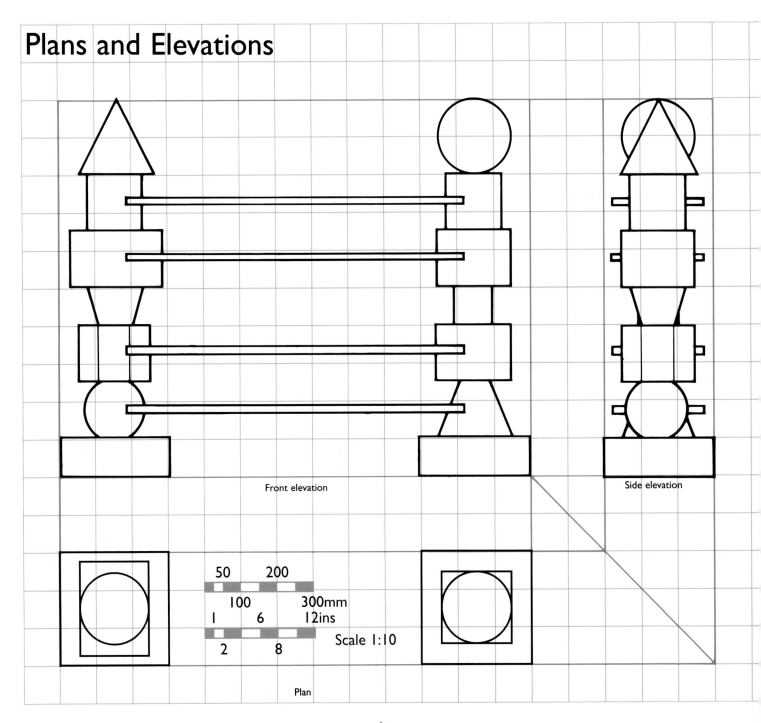

Front elevation

Side elevation

50   200

100   300mm
1   6   12ins
2   8   Scale 1:10

Plan

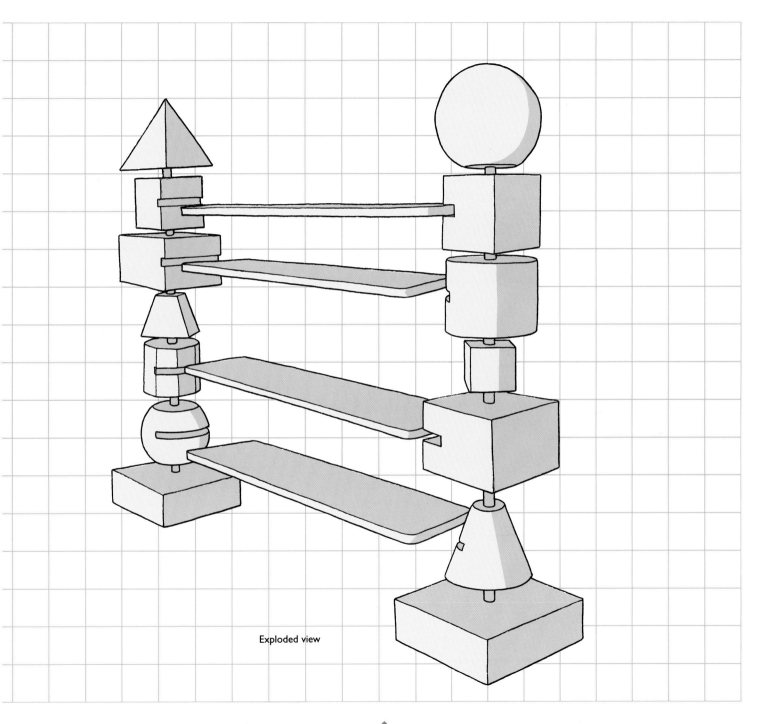

Exploded view

The supports

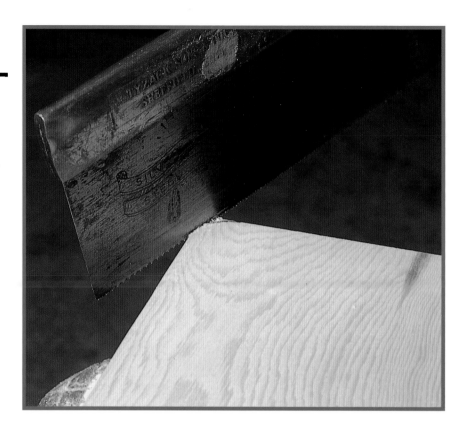

1 Make the first set of parts – the two support poles and bases. Cut some plywood or particle board to make the top and four sides of a five-sided box; construct these using a similar method to that used to make the drawer holders shown in the storage unit. Mark the center of the top face and drill a hole that will accept the pole. Using some of the softwood scraps, glue a stack of approximately 6 inches over the hole and, when the glue is dry, continue drilling the hole to a predetermined depth, making sure that it is precisely vertical. Then glue the support pole in place in the hole and sand ready for finishing.

2 Now make the shelves. Prepare the wood to the correct size – length, width, and thickness. Plane and sand smooth to ensure a good surface. Since some of the corners of the shelves project from the solids, it is advisable to round the corners. Use a washer or other appropriately sized disk and draw the curve.

3 Saw off the corner before rounding with a plane, chisel, or rasp. After a final sanding, the shelves are ready for finishing.

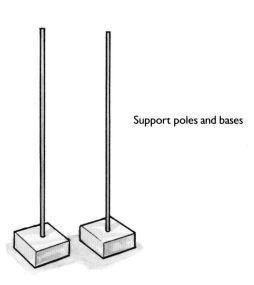

Support poles and bases

4 Next make the shapes. These were made by gluing together pieces of wood as it is unlikely that you will find solid wood of a large enough size, and if you did, you could not be sure if it was dry or stable enough. By laminating the blocks, you can be sure of the moisture content and gain greater stability. Cut the boards into standard lengths from which the shapes can be cut, allowing at least 2¾ inches of waste on the end for final trimming. Apply glue to the faces to be joined. To prevent these lengths from slipping out of place when you apply the clamps, partially insert a nail as a location.

5 Apply enough clamps to give the required pressure and leave the glue to dry.

6 When the glue has cured, plane the long-grain faces square and saw the end-grain faces square. It is unsafe to try to make this cut in one pass, and it is unlikely that most home woodworkers would have a circular saw large enough. So, make a cut one-third deep on the four faces, using a fence to guide the work. Then finish the cut with a handsaw. Make enough of these blocks to complete the required number of shapes.

7 Cut the shapes to their overall sizes and proceed to lay out, cut, and shape each piece. Before starting the final shaping, it is wise to cut the slots that will receive the shelves. It is safer to make these cuts while the blocks are square. Make two parallel sawcuts that will give a slot of the required width. *Note:* The guard has been removed for photographic clarity, but this is not recommended in general practice. Remove the waste with a chisel of a smaller or equivalent width.

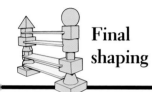

Final shaping

8 Some of the geometric solids are simple adaptations of a rectangular block; some need further elaborate cutting and shaping. The basic block is rectangular, and from this a cube can easily be cut. It is simple to lay out an octagon on a cube and then cut off and plane the four new faces.

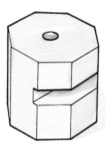 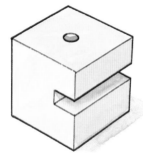

Shaped blocks

9 Mark the center on all the shapes and drill a hole to accept the support pole.

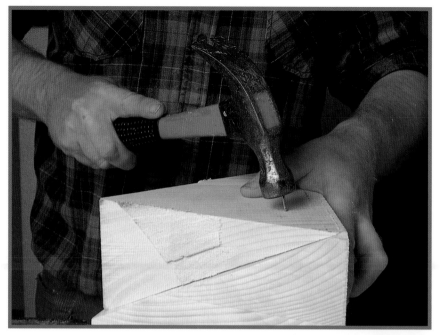

10 A pyramid can be made in a similar way to the truncated solid. Since the top comes to a point, once the first cut is made, it is safer to nail the waste scrap piece back in place so that the next side can be cut safely. Keep your hands away from the saw blade.

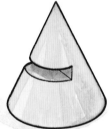

11 Other shapes may need to be turned, but the cylinder can be made either way. Mark the center and use a compass or trammel to mark the circumference.

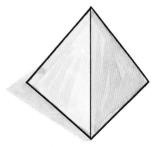

12 It is possible to cut this cylinder on a bandsaw and then plane and sand the edges smooth or, having sawn off most of the waste, to place the block in a lathe and turn it to a cylinder.

13 To make a sphere or cone, mark the center and cut as for a cylinder, but then turn the required shape. The cone is simply a matter of turning a straight line from the cylindrical base to its tip. The sphere needs to be turned, so carefully shape the block from a cylinder to the final shape in stages. It is a good idea to make a cardboard template of the sphere which can be used to check the progress of the turning. Gradually round the ends of the block to create a sphere.

Finishing

14 All the shapes will need filling (especially the end grain) and sanding in preparation for finishing. Apply a primer/filler coat to all the components to be colored and decorated (the shapes and the base). Apply clear or colored finish to the shelves and leave the support posts unfinished.

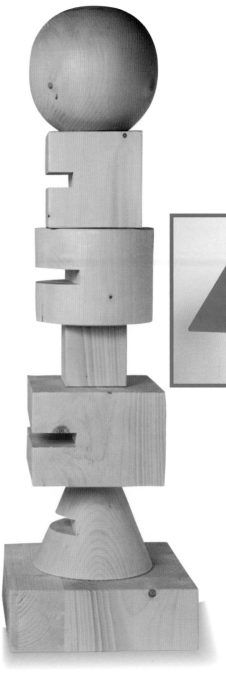

15 When the primer is dry, paint and decorate. Aerosol spray paints will produce a good finish if you follow the instructions on the can. Mount each solid on a pole to spray different colors. Finally, assemble the stacks of solids onto the poles, position the shelves, and the system is ready to use.

16 This very colorful and practical unit has the added advantage of being completely adjustable. You and your children will have great fun rearranging the supporting blocks.

Stacks of Shelves

The initial project uses wooden blocks cut to the the various platonic solids and painted. Once you have made the starting blocks, try turning them to different shapes from those used in the photographs, making sure that the slots for the shelves remain lined up.

Building Blocks Here the original blocks are kept the same shape as in the project, but letters have been painted on them. You can, of course, use numbers or, as shown in the alternative examples for the toybox, spell out your child's name. Don't forget that the shelves are adjustable and that the blocks can be repositioned to spell different words.

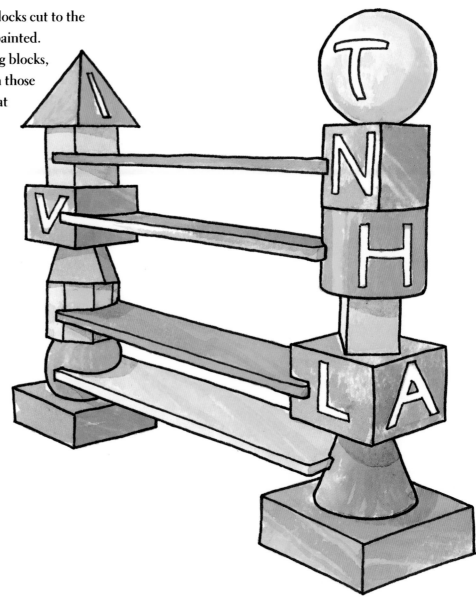

The Chess Set Here the shapes are a little more complex, but a theme based on these chess pieces works very well. Why not try the carving technique (shown later for making the animal bed project) for the horse's head of the chess knight? For something a little less ambitious, you could model the blocks on checkers, similar to those shown below in the natural-look shelves.

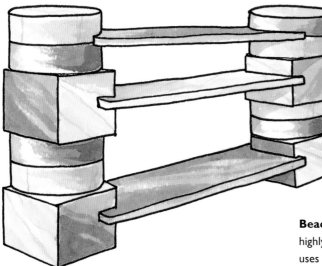

The Natural Look If a reasonable match of the wood grain is achieved, the shapes can be left natural and simply varnished. Again, though, don't forget that you can vary the shapes of the blocks and the number of shelves.

Beach Balls This fun and highly colorful variation uses beach balls and buckets in a balancing act. It could even follow on from the circus theme used in other projects.

8

Humpty Dumpty Stool and Chair

These pieces make an interesting set using the theme of Humpty Dumpty in an original way. The techniques include turning to produce the legs and rails, and to apply the nursery rhyme decorative shaping. The stool is very simple, and if you are not used to turning, try this first. The chair, like the stool, is made with a solid wood seat. Most of the other parts are cylindrical, many with turned decoration. These pieces are beautifully finished and made to last.

TOOLS

Hand	Power	Machine	Function
Lathe gouges and chisels		lathe	turn parts
Hand/coping saw	jigsaw	bandsaw	cut parts
Plane	electric plane	surfacer/ thicknesser	plane seats
Bar clamps			assembly
Band/web clamps			assembly
Hand drill	electric drill	drill press	drill holes
Assorted twist-drill, auger, spade or forstner bits			drill holes
Calipers			check turning diameter
Spokeshaves	router		apply small rounds
Screwdriver			insert screws
Hammer			insert wedges
Chisel			trim wedges
Brushes	spray gun		apply finish

CUTTING LIST

Part	No.	Length	Width	Thickness
From solid wood				
Stool seat	1		9in dia.	1in
Stool legs	4	9in		1¾in dia.
Chair seat	1	11¾in	11in (taper to 9⅛in)	¾in
Back legs	2	26¼in		1⅜in dia.
Front legs	2	12⅝in		1⅜in dia.
Top back rail	1	9in	1¾in	¾in
Lower back rails	2	9in		1in dia.
Lower front to back rails	4	9⅝in		⅝in dia.
Lower crossrails	2	9in		1in dia. (taper to ⅝in)
Soldier back slats	3	6¾in		1⅛in diam.

Plus: Glue, clear finish, paints, sandpaper, posterboard/plywood for templates.

Plans and Elevations

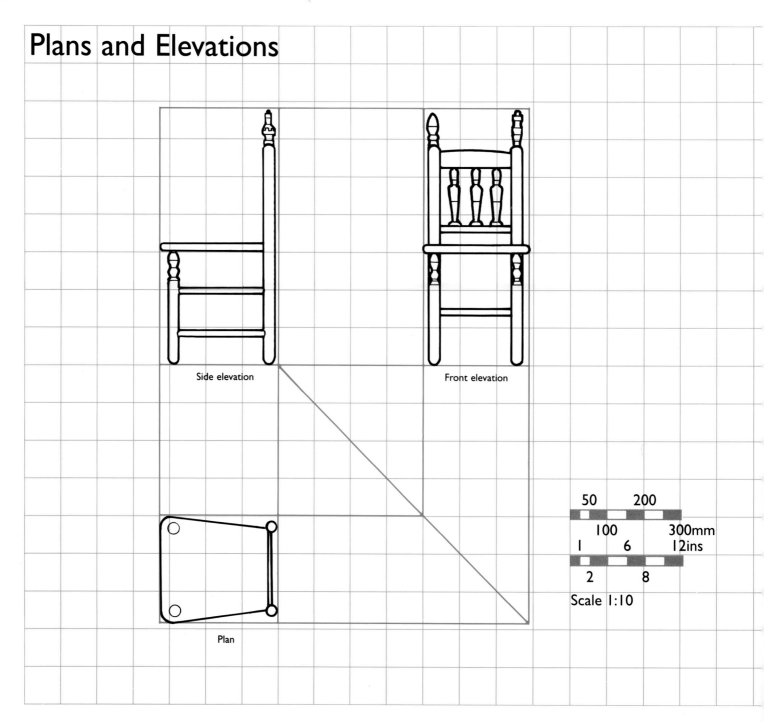

Side elevation

Front elevation

Plan

50   200
100   300mm
1   6   12ins
2   8

Scale 1:10

Templates

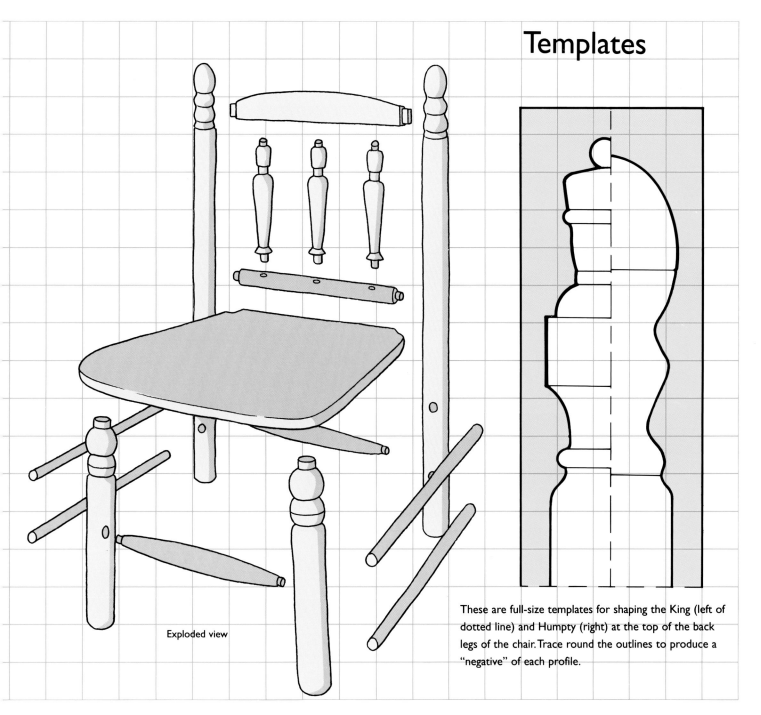

Exploded view

These are full-size templates for shaping the King (left of dotted line) and Humpty (right) at the top of the back legs of the chair. Trace round the outlines to produce a "negative" of each profile.

Plans and Elevations

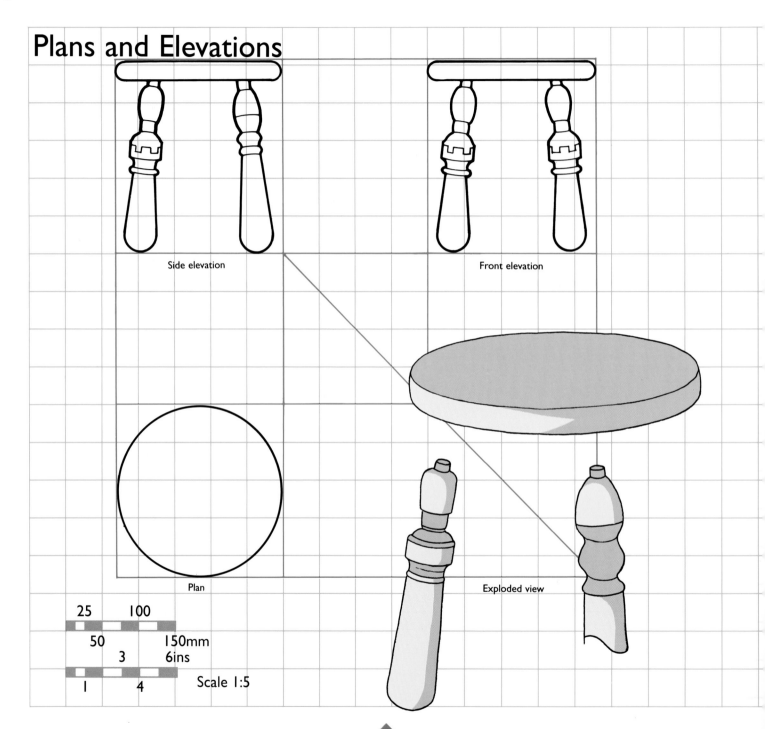

Side elevation

Front elevation

Plan

Exploded view

25   100
50   150mm
3   6ins
1   4   Scale 1:5

Templates

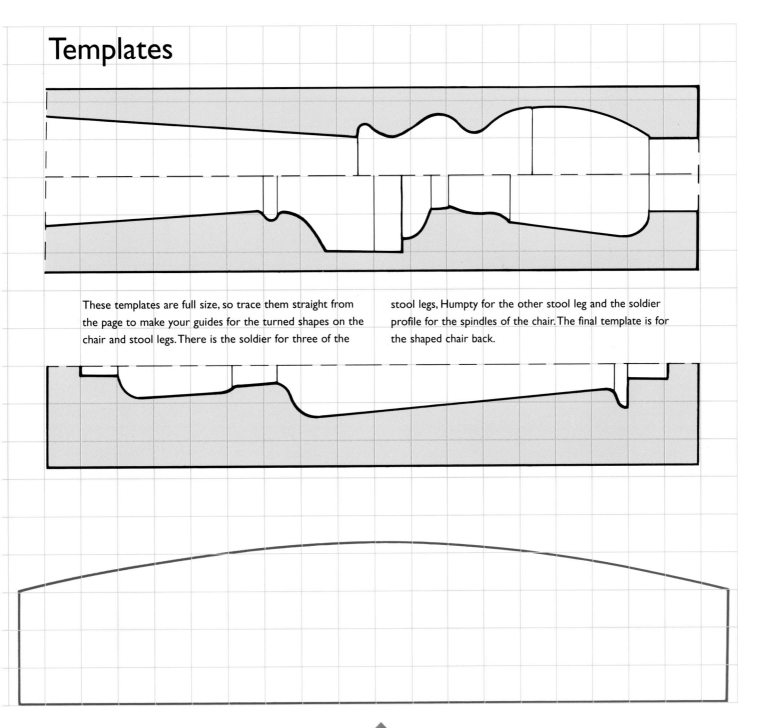

These templates are full size, so trace them straight from the page to make your guides for the turned shapes on the chair and stool legs. There is the soldier for three of the stool legs, Humpty for the other stool leg and the soldier profile for the spindles of the chair. The final template is for the shaped chair back.

The stool seat

1 The seat is made from natural wood which may need to be glued from smaller pieces if the width is not available. This procedure is illustrated in the rocking chair project (page 68).

Draw the circle for the seat and cut it out with a jigsaw or bandsaw. You can use a jigsaw or router like a compass to make this cut.

2 It is good practice to round off a small curve on the edges of the disk, which can be achieved by using a router with a suitable bit. These processes can, of course, be carried out using hand tools if you do not have machines. A spokeshave will enable you to smooth the cut edge and to apply the round.

3 Now mark the positions for the four legs using a compass or a set of dividers. Draw the radius of the circle on which the leg centers will lie and mark the four points.

Making the stool legs

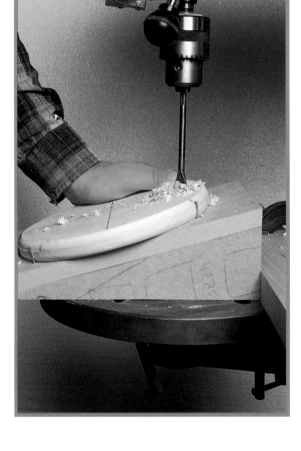

4 The legs splay out; to achieve this, you will need to drill the holes at an angle. Make a jig that will hold the seat at the correct angle to the vertical drill press and drill the four holes.

5 Now make the four legs. This is where you will use the lathe. Cut the wood to be turned slightly over final length, and mark the centers of the wood at each end. Marks from the four corners giving diagonal lines will achieve an exact center.

Fit the wood into the lathe; the left-hand end is the driving end, from motor to wood, and the other end simply runs free. Now take the turning gouge or chisel and make careful cuts to remove the corners of the wood. Continue turning until the leg is round.

6 During the process of turning, check that you are nearing the required diameter. You can use calipers set to the required measurement for this when the lathe has stopped.

7 Having turned the cylindrical leg, turn the shapes for the decoration. The first stage is to do some shaping by eye, in this case for the "Humpty" shape. Make sure when turning the ends of the legs that they will fit exactly into the holes that you have drilled in the seat.

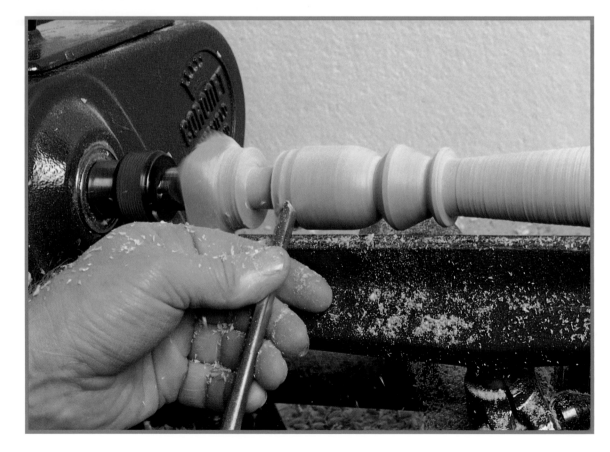

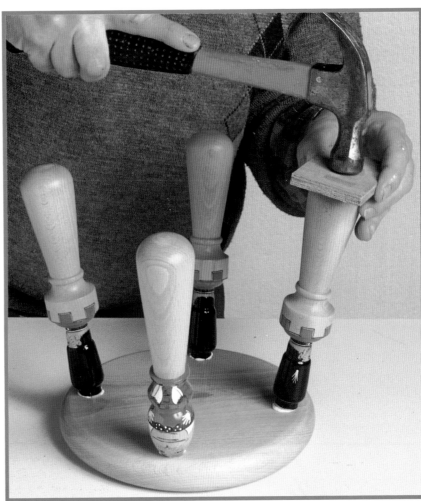

8 Now, using the appropriate template, check that the shaping is correct. Use the calipers to check the diameter of the ends. Continue to shape the three other "soldier" legs and sand these parts as shown in step 11. You can then paint the four legs following the sequence on page 136 before assembly.

9 The legs can now be attached to the seat. Apply glue to the ends of the legs and fit into the holes. Either drill the holes so that they do not come through the top, or drill through and wedge the legs in place. If you decide on the latter, you will have a stronger joint. Remember to make a sawcut in the end of the legs and hammer in wedges from the top.

This process is shown in the chair sequence. Chisel the wedges flat and smooth with sandpaper (see step 23).

CROSS REFERENCE

Wood turning	12
Using templates	9
Joints	14

Making the chair

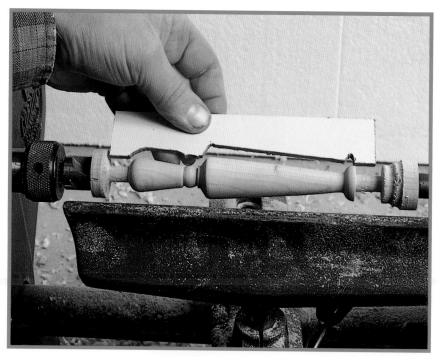

10 Make the turned parts in the same way as you did for the stool, shaping by eye and then using a template to make sure of the exact shape required. This is the "soldier" for one back leg, but you will also need to shape the "King" on the other back legs and the three spindles as soldiers for the back. Turn the ends of each decoration to the correct size to fit in the crossrails, checking again with calipers.

11 Finally, check that you have the shape you require and sand the turned parts. In order to work safely, place the sandpaper behind the work, holding it from the underneath by its edge. Then use your other hand simply to guide the sandpaper from the back onto the revolving work. Never try to grip – just press lightly on the sheet of sandpaper, which is held safely in your other hand, well below the turning wood.

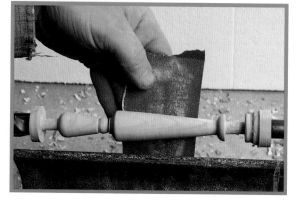

12 Check that you have made all the parts. There should be: 1 back frame comprising: 2 back legs with Humpty and the King turned at the top, 1 rectangular top rail, 3 turned soldier spindles, and 1 turned crossrail; another turned crossrail at the bottom under the seat; 2 front legs with some turning just under the seat; 2 sets of 2 rails from the back legs to the front legs; 1 crossrail between the front legs; 1 solid seat.

Drilling the holes

13 Drill holes in the front and back legs to receive the turned crossrails. Make a jig so that the turned pieces fit securely and are held safely in place while you drill the holes.

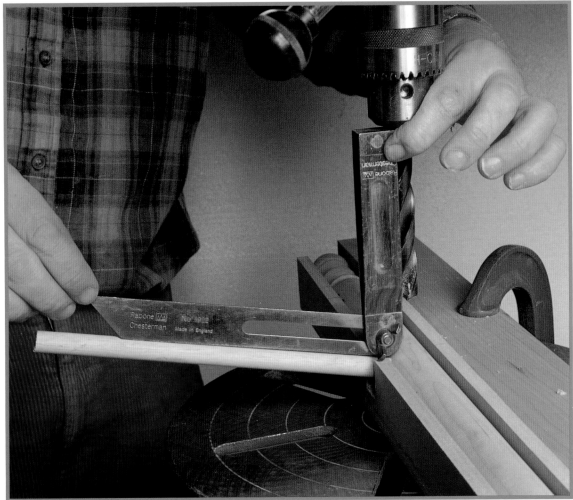

14 When drilling the back legs, having first drilled the rails that go across to make the back frame, you will then need to drill holes for the rails that go from back to front, making sure that they are at the correct angle to those you have already drilled. You need to adapt your jig in this case so that you can put a temporary dowel in the holes that you have drilled, then align the work with the drill so that the second holes are at the correct angle. When this drilling is done, try assembling the chair dry, making sure all parts fit, and make any adjustments as necessary.

Painting

15 Before assembling the chair, apply the finish to the three soldiers in the back slat using the following painting sequence: tunic; trousers; bearskin hat; feet; white belt, and facial features. These are much easier to paint when they are separate pieces than when assembled.

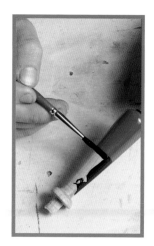

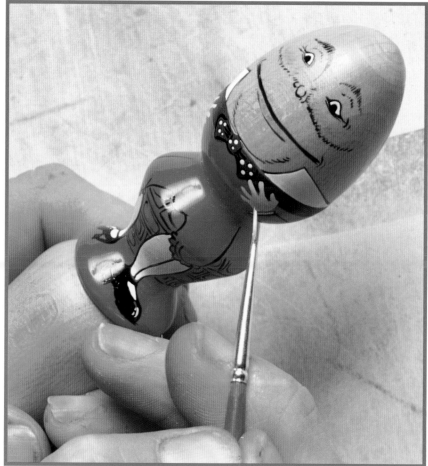

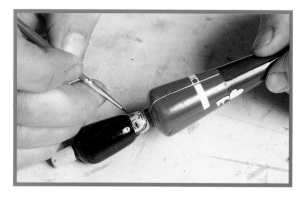

16 The two decorative turnings at the top of the back legs – Humpty and the King – can be painted before or after assembly.

Assembly

17 It is customary in chair making to assemble the back frame first. Make the section comprising the top back rail, three turned soldiers, and bottom turned rail. Apply glue to the holes and assemble these parts.

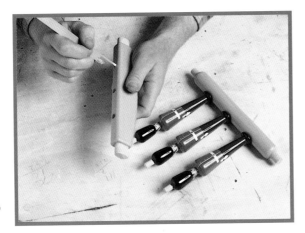

18 Now assemble the complete back using bar clamps, making sure that the whole frame is square.

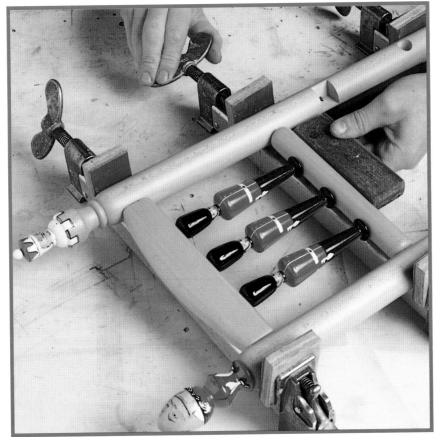

19 Assemble the two front legs and the front crossrail together and glue in position at the seat front. As before, hold the assembly in bar clamps.

20 In order to attach the front legs to the seat, the legs project through the seat and are wedged in place. At this stage, hammer in wedges.

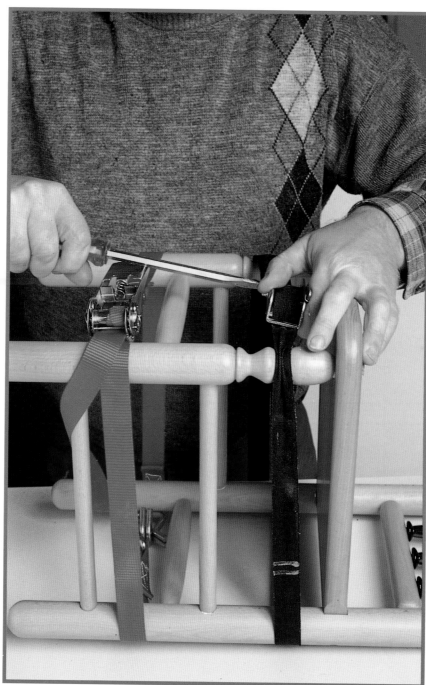

21 When the glue for this assembly has dried, place the seat and front-to-back rails in position, having first applied glue. This assembly can now be clamped using band or web clamps.

22 The seat sits in a small groove in the back legs; reinforce this joint by screwing through from the outside of the back leg into the seat. Recess the screw into the leg, and insert a plug to hide it.

23 Now the chair is assembled, other general finishing can be carried out. Earlier we glued wedges when assembling the front legs to the seat. Chisel them flat, then smooth with sandpaper. Finally, check the chair all over and apply the final finish. Wipe with flat varnish and then apply wax-polish. The same finish can be applied to the stool.

Sitting Pretty

Although the original project was made using the theme of Humpty Dumpty, other nursery rhymes or stories would work just as well, as shown by these examples. These illustrations show the adaptations on the chair, but they can also apply to the matching stool.

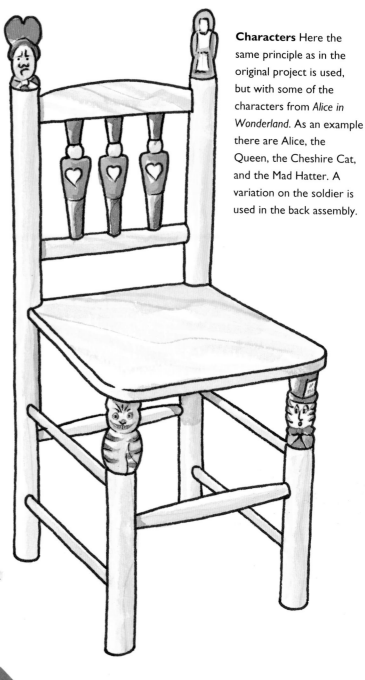

Characters Here the same principle as in the original project is used, but with some of the characters from *Alice in Wonderland*. As an example there are Alice, the Queen, the Cheshire Cat, and the Mad Hatter. A variation on the soldier is used in the back assembly.

Cutouts and Colors As with the cradle, you can also use cutouts—numbers and letters in bold colors. This approach also works well with geometric shapes similar to those in the shelving system. Paint the child's name on the shaped blocks on the back. Another colorful option is the balancing balls alternative, also shown for the shelving system.

Planets This is a simple but effective addition to the spacecraft theme on the following page. Turn the top of the leg to form a sphere and then paint it to look like Earth or one of the other planets.

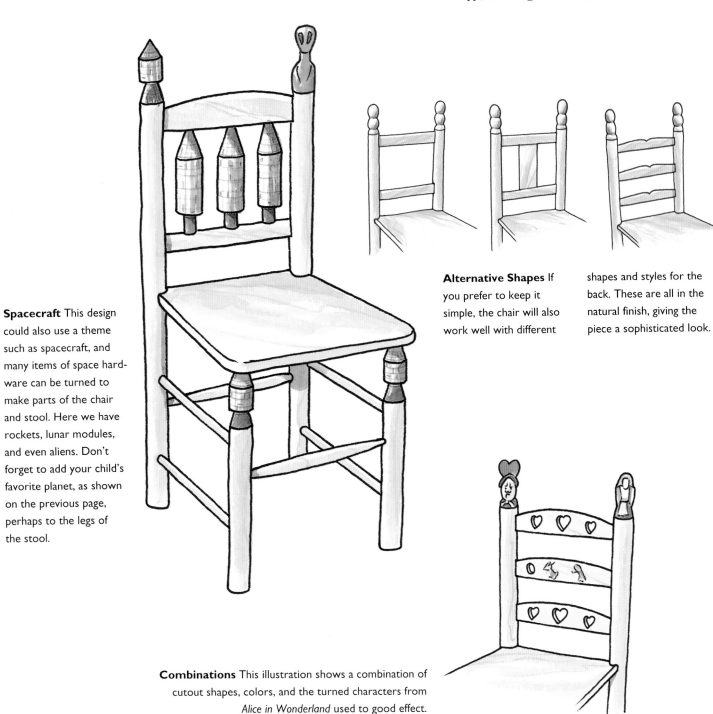

Spacecraft This design could also use a theme such as spacecraft, and many items of space hardware can be turned to make parts of the chair and stool. Here we have rockets, lunar modules, and even aliens. Don't forget to add your child's favorite planet, as shown on the previous page, perhaps to the legs of the stool.

Alternative Shapes If you prefer to keep it simple, the chair will also work well with different shapes and styles for the back. These are all in the natural finish, giving the piece a sophisticated look.

Combinations This illustration shows a combination of cutout shapes, colors, and the turned characters from *Alice in Wonderland* used to good effect.

9

Wild Animal Bed

The design of this piece is an interesting and original departure from a bed. It is basically composed of two carvings of an animal, in this case, a leopard. The cats stand on each side of the bed with a baseboard between them to support the mattress. The headboard is held between the two tails. You could, of course, adapt this design and choose a different four-legged animal of approximately the same pro-

portions, but an elephant probably would not be suitable.

The construction of this bed is similar to the shelving system (see page 110), but on a larger scale. It is made from gluing cabinet-grade softwood together to form the outline of the wood block from which the detail is then carved.

Hand	Power	Machine	Function
Bar clamps/C-clamps			assembly
Brace/wheelbrace and drill bits	electric drill	drill press	drill dowel holes
Panel and coping saws	jigsaw	bandsaw	cut lengths and shapes
Carving gouges	wood grinder		carving
Carving mallet	router		grooving
Brushes			finish and decoration
Blow lamp			decoration

CUTTING LIST

Part	No.	Length	Width	Thickness
From 3in cabinet-grade softwood				
Main spine	2	7ft 2½in	6in	2¾in
Legs	8	24in	4½in	2¾in
Heads	2	17in	9in	2¾in
Tails	4	2ft 7in	5in	2¾in
Use scraps for thickening at shoulder, flanks, and legs.				

From plywood				
Headboard	1	2ft 7½in	2ft	⅜in
Headboard curved battens	2	23⅜in	2in	⅝in
Perforated base	1	6ft 4½in	3ft	¾in
Crossrails	3			
Plus: Glue, sandpaper, dowels, primer, paints.				

Plans and Elevations

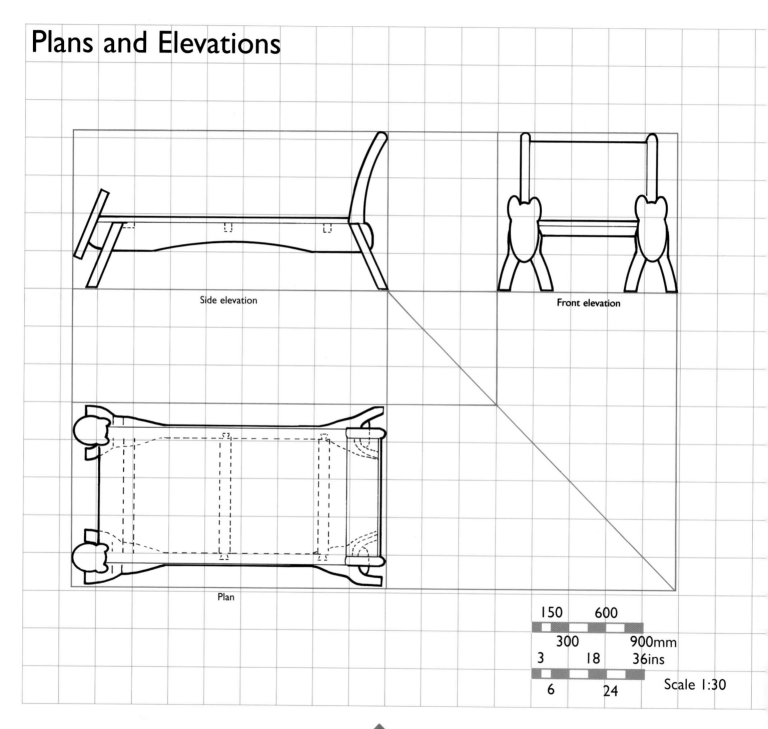

Side elevation

Front elevation

Plan

150   600
300   900mm
3   18   36ins
6   24   Scale 1:30

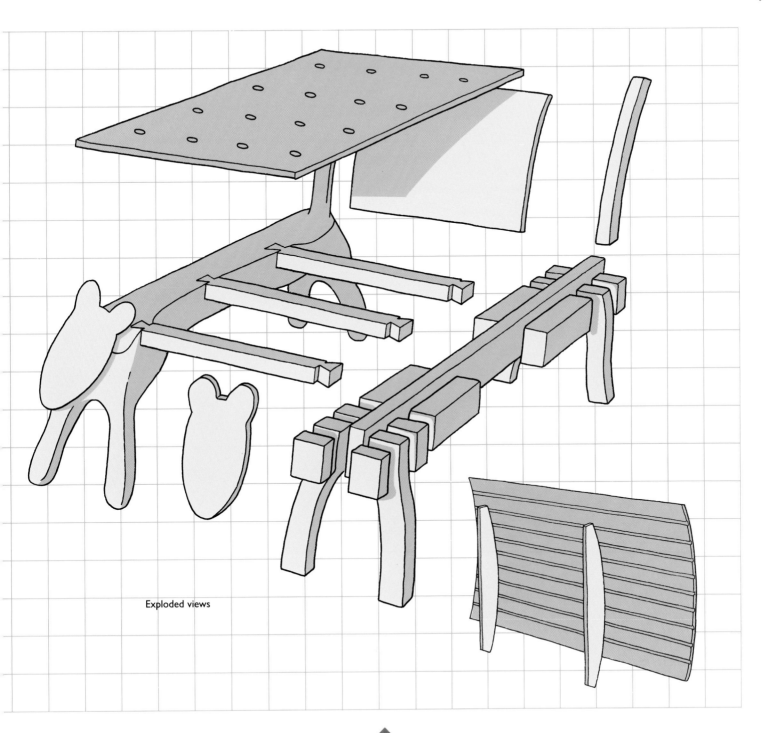

Exploded views

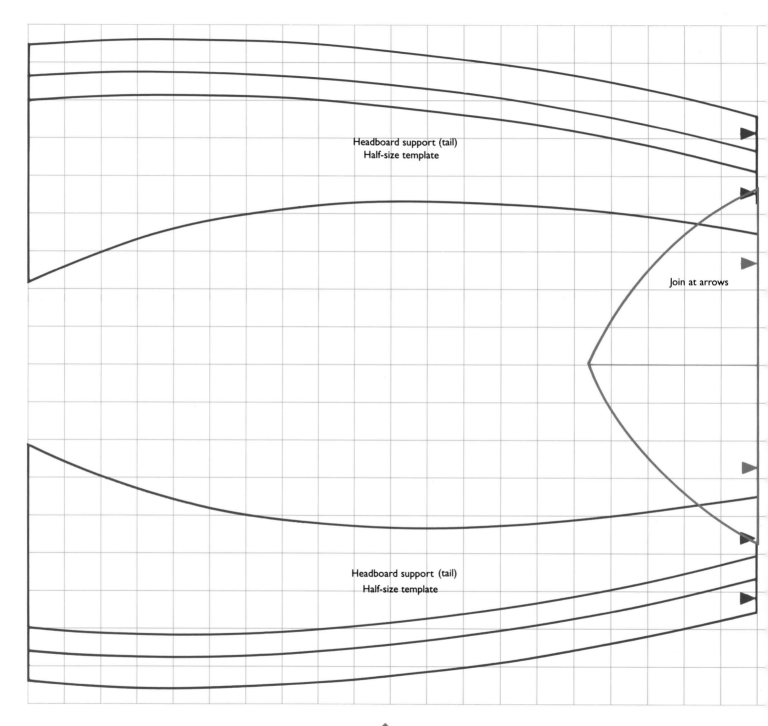

Headboard support (tail)
Half-size template

Join at arrows

Headboard support (tail)
Half-size template

Templates

Scale these templates up or use them straight from the page to make the heads and tails.

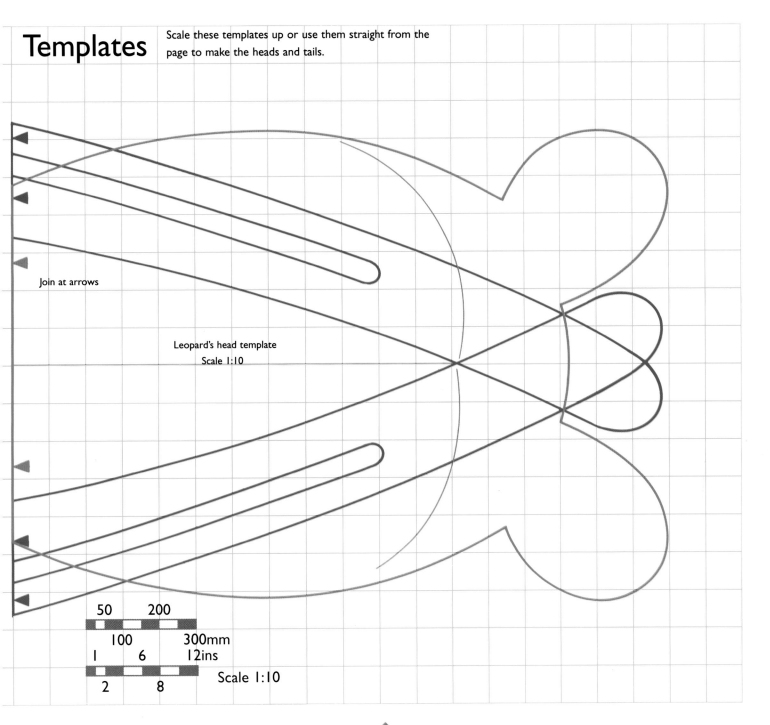

Join at arrows

Leopard's head template
Scale 1:10

50		200	
100		300mm	
1	6	12ins	
2	8		

Scale 1:10

Cutting the shapes

1 First assemble the parts for each of the two cats – a long piece for the main body, four legs, a head, a tail, and other blocks shown in the illustrations to thicken and build the shapes of the body and limbs. Cut the inside curve first to give the legs their correct stance.

3 Once you have a good fit, apply the glue and clamp the blocks in place.

2 Add the blocks that make the shoulders to the front of the legs, and start fitting the flanks behind the legs.

4 The outsides of the legs are curved, so you need to use the pieces of waste from the insides of the legs and glue and clamp them to the outsides of the legs.

5 Cut an angled recess in both sides of the main body piece at the rear, and glue and clamp both legs in position.

6 Cut two more thickening pieces for the back legs and glue and clamp these in position as before. At this stage the animal consists of a plank for the back with four legs and some local thickening attached.

The head and tail

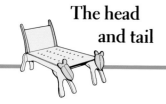

7 Next, lay out the head and tail. You can either use your own design drawn directly on the wood or trace around a template. Carefully cut out the shape.

8 Now cut the tail, which is curved, and rout a groove parallel to the curved front edge. Remember that this groove needs to be on the inside when the two animals are standing together, so that the headboard can be secured in place. Note

the adaptation of a straight fence to enable you to rout parallel with a curved component. In this case, two pieces of dowel are cut in half to make two half rounds and attached to the fence to enable the machine to follow a curve.

9 Complete this groove and put the two tails to one side to be attached later.

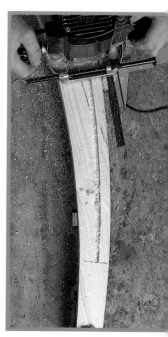

Shaping the body

10 The photographs show the use of a fairly recently developed power carving tool. It is similar to an angle grinder but has a special cutter that fits in place of the grinding wheel. If you decide to use this, remember that great care must be taken. Always make sure that both you and the work are securely placed and stable, and wear goggles to protect your eyes from splinters and dust. If you do not have such a tool, you can use carving gouges throughout. Carve major waste from the blocks and continue carving to bring the shape as close as possible to the one you wish to achieve.

11 You will see that it is useful not to have the tail in position at this stage, since the body can be turned in all directions to allow you to work more easily.

12 Continue with this shaping and then follow the same basic procedure for the head.

13 If you are using the power carving tool, stop when the roughing out is near the final shape and carry out the final carving with a gouge. At this stage you have more control to achieve a really fine finish; let the gouge marks be a part of the surface texture and decoration. Work in the same way on the head as you have with the body.

14 To secure the head to the body, mark the position of the dowels between the body and head. Drill the holes and insert the dowels.

15 If necessary, clean up the edges at this point with a plane. Now glue the head in place.

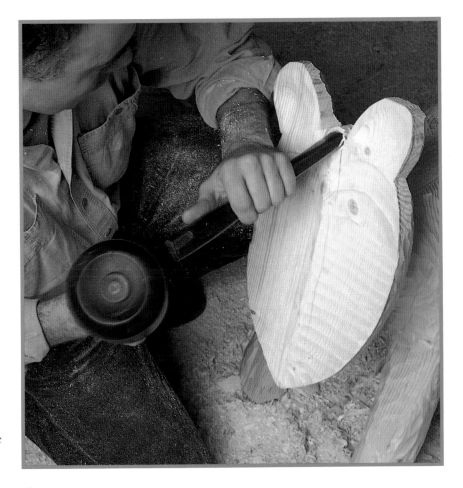

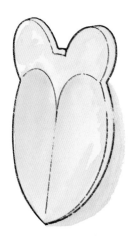

Shaped face

16 When the glue has dried, carry out some final carving with the grinder and use gouges until the front is finished.

17 When all the carving is complete, you can attach the tail in place. A way of making sure the dowels are in the correct position is to put some brads on one joint face to locate the brads in position; gently press both faces together and the brads will give you an exact positioning on the opposing face.

18 Remove the brads and drill the holes to accept the dowels. Put the dowels in the holes and glue the tail in position. You now have two cats ready to decorate.

20 Decorate the headboard by etching a design of your choice on the surface and then painting over it.

19 Make the headboard from a sheet of plywood. Cut a series of lateral grooves on the reverse side to make it easier to bend the wood. Cut two tapered curved battens and glue and clamp these in position on the plywood to hold the curve of the headboard.

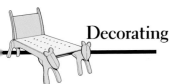

Decorating

21 Paint the base coat, in this case yellow, on the body and face; continue until you have painted both animals completely. Now add the details.

22 An interesting effect can be achieved by using a small blowtorch to scorch the surface to create the animal's spots.

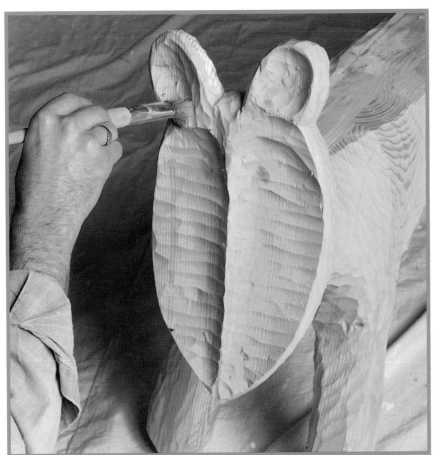

23 Alternatively, you can use paint to apply the markings and any facial features.

Assembly

24 To link the cross rails of the bed, first make a lapped dovetail where each crossrail joins the sides and cut with a saw. Then remove the waste by drilling out and chiseling to the marked lines.

25 Drill and countersink screw holes in the crossrails, then slot the crossrails into the sides of the animal supports. Slot the headboard into the grooves between the tails.

27 The completed assembly should be extremely solid and sturdy at this stage.

28 Lay a perforated sheet of hardboard on the crossrails, add some cozy bedding, and you'll soon persuade even your most boisterous child that it's bedtime.

26 Now secure the assembly firmly using very long screws or bolts through the rails and the body supports.

Beautiful Beds

This project was based on a leopard but there are many other animals that your child could choose. Experiment with different body shapes and sizes. This is a full-size single bed, but if space is limited, you can always scale it down to a smaller size to suit a younger child.

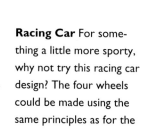

Racing Car For something a little more sporty, why not try this racing car design? The four wheels could be made using the same principles as for the shelving unit, with recesses for the bed support. Then you can decorate the headboard in your child's favorite colors.

Ancient Egypt Following the theme used in projects like the storage unit, this sphinx design works well, and a lot can be done by painting pyramids on the headboard to reinforce the theme. Don't forget to adapt the feet of the bed to whatever design you choose, as shown in the three examples on this page.

Alligator This variation on the animal theme means a subtle change of body shape to a more squat design for an alligator or crocodile. This approach gives you an opportunity not only to change the decoration for the body, but also to try out different shapes for the feet.

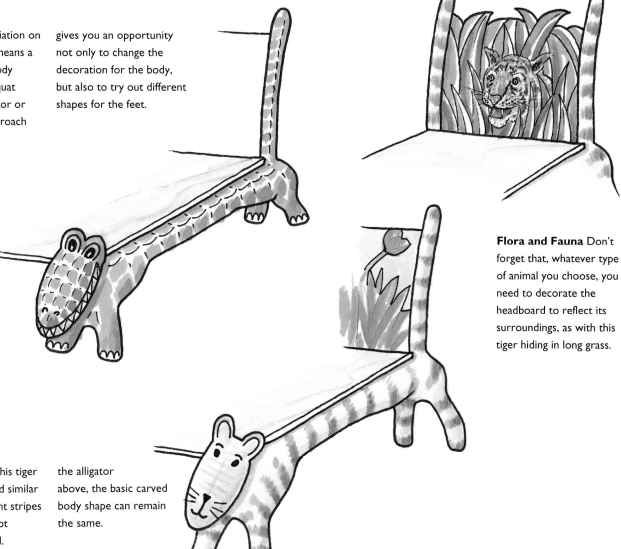

Flora and Fauna Don't forget that, whatever type of animal you choose, you need to decorate the headboard to reflect its surroundings, as with this tiger hiding in long grass.

More Big Cats This tiger design is simple and similar to the original. Paint stripes instead of spots, not forgetting the head. Another alternative is a cheetah, with blotches rather than spots or stripes. This way, unlike the alligator above, the basic carved body shape can remain the same.

10

Circus Armoire

This design is a fresh approach for a child wanting more than traditional closet. The piece consists of a base cabinet and drawers; four uprights containing three panels and a fitted curtain door; a top frame holding 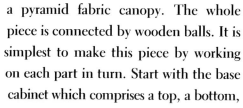 a pyramid fabric canopy. The whole piece is connected by wooden balls. It is simplest to make this piece by working on each part in turn. Start with the base cabinet which comprises a top, a bottom, two sides with grooves, and a back.

TOOLS

Hand	Power	Machine	Function
Panel saw	circular/jigsaw	radial arm saw/	
		table saw	cut panels
Plane	electric plane	surfacer/	
		thicknesser	plane materials
Plow or rabbet plane	router		cut grooves
	Biscuit jointer		make carcass joints
	(or make routered grooves and use plywood tongues)		
Mallet and hammer			fit joints
Bar clamps			clamp joints
Wheelbrace/brace	electric drill	drill press	drill holes
Twist drill, auger or spade bits,			
twist bits, forstner bits			drill holes
		lathe	turn spheres (or purchase already turned)
Screwdriver			insert screws
Brushes		spray gun	apply finish

CUTTING LIST

Part	No.	Length	Width	Thickness
From manufactured board				
Base cabinet top	1	21½in	20½in	⅝in
Cabinet bottom	1	21½in	21½in	⅝in
Cabinet sides	2	21in	14½in	⅝in
Cabinet back	1	19¾in	14½in	⅝in
Drawer bases	3	19⅛in	17⅞in	¼in
Drawer sides	6	20½in	4½in	½in
Drawer backs	3	17⅞in	4½in	½in
Drawer fronts	3	18½in	4½in	½in
False drawer fronts	3	20in	4½in	⅝in

Part	No	Length	Width	Thickness
From solid wood				
Base cabinet lippings	6	21½in	1¼in	⅝in
Drawer runner inserts	6	21in	1⅛in	⅜in
Drawer runners	6	20½in	⅝in	⅜in
Side curved uprights	4	4ft 7⅝in	1⅝in	1⅜in
Top frame main members	4	2ft 7½in	2¼in	1⅝in
Top frame pyramid sides	4	1ft 7in	⅝in	½in
Frame central boss	1	2½in		2½in diam.
Balls	9	2½in diam.		
Hanging rail	1	27½in		⅞in diam.
Rail supports	2	4in	2½in	¾in

Part	No	Length	Width	Thickness
From plywood				
Side panels	2	4ft 8in	1ft 8⅜in	¼in
Back panel	1	4ft 8in	27⅞in/20⅜in (top/bottom)	¼in

Plus: Offcuts of 15mm (⅝in) MDF for handles, offcuts of 22mm (⅞in) dowel for handle supports, 6mm (¼in) chromed stee rod, curtain rings, fabric, glue, screws/male threaded inserts, female threaded inserts, clear lacquer, paints, abrasive paper, biscuits joints or ply tongues.

Plans and Elevations

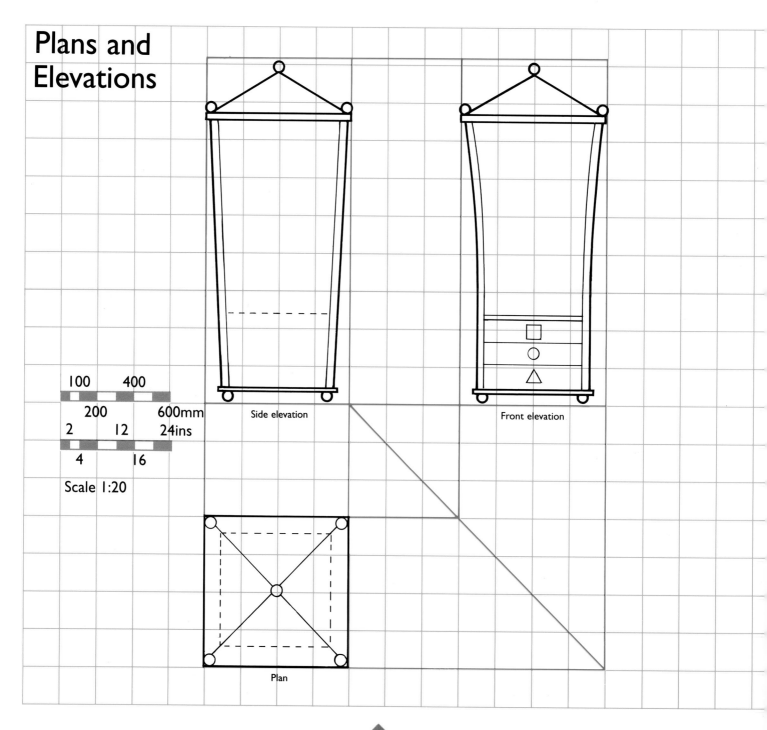

100   400

200   600mm

2   12   24ins

4   16

Scale 1:20

Side elevation

Front elevation

Plan

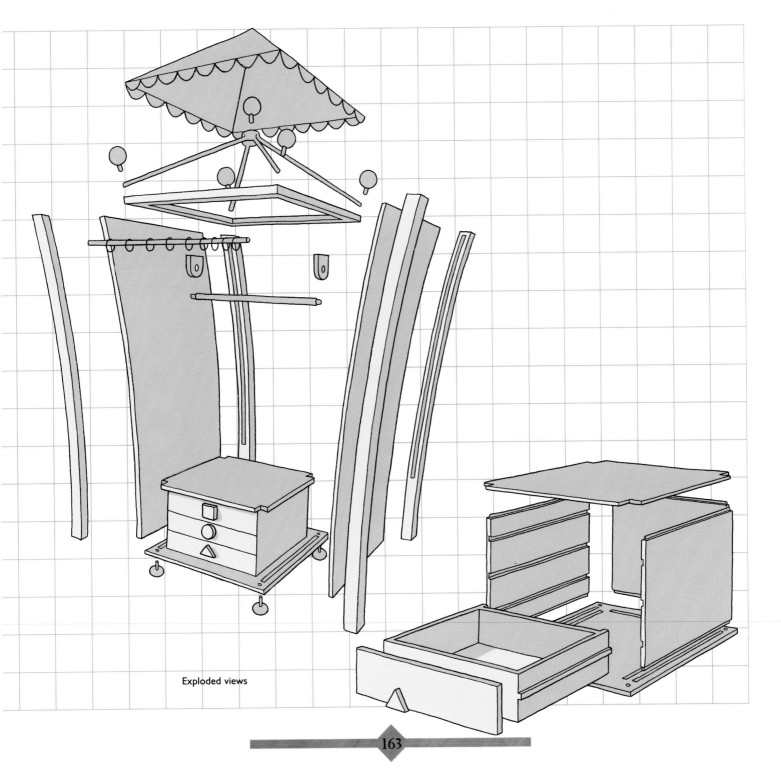

Exploded views

The base cabinet

1 First lay out the parts on the board material, using a T-square against a straight edge and marking with pencil and ruler.

2 The top and bottom are made from manufactured board – in this case fiberboard – and have solid wood edgings on some edges. The top has edgings on the front and back, while the bottom has edgings all around. Prepare these two parts first by making a groove in the edge of the board where an edging will be attached.

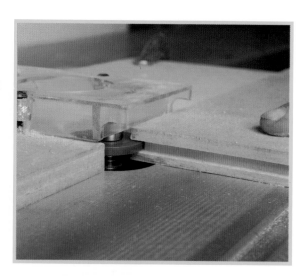

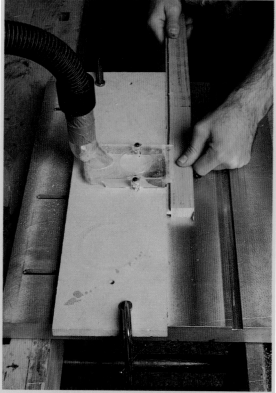

3 Then machine the solid edging to make a tongue that will fit into this groove.

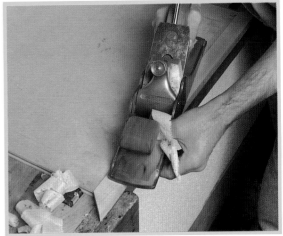

4 Mark the solid wood to length, allowing for a miter on each of the four corners. These can be cut either from the saw or, for greater accuracy, trim using a miter shooting board with a plane.

5 Now glue the edgings onto the fiberboard and clamp in place.

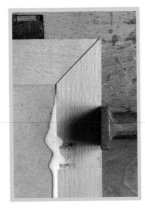

6 When the glue is dry, plane the edging flush with the board, noting that the overall dimension of the top is smaller than that of the bottom.

The sides and back

7 The back is plain, but the sides need grooves in them into which the drawer runners will fit. It is generally not advisable to place drawer runners directly in manufactured board, so insert strips of solid wood into the board face where the grooves for the drawer runners will be cut. Start by making a series of routered cuts to accept these solid strips.

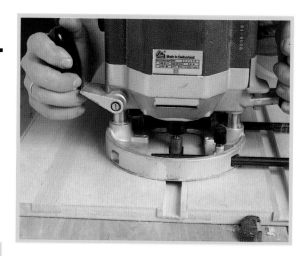

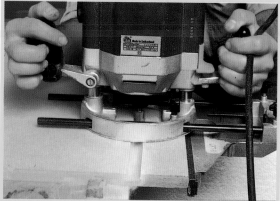

9 Now rout the grooves into these strips to take the drawer runners in the correct position.

8 Then apply glue to the groove and tap in the strips. When the glue is dry, plane these strips flush with the fiberboard face.

10 The cabinet is connected with biscuit joints, so make the necessary slots in the top and bottom edges of the sides and back.

11 Make the corresponding slots in the inside faces of the top and bottom and, at the same time, make a groove in the bottom that will accept the side and back panels. When this is complete, check the whole assembly dry and, if all is well, prepare for final assembly.

13 Now assemble the bottom, top, two sides, and back, making sure that the cabinet is square when the joints are clamped.

12 Place the biscuits in their slots and apply glue to the joint area. Note that a hole has been drilled at the corners which will secure the uprights.

The drawers

14 Now make the drawers to fit into the cabinet. These can be made in fiberboard in a similar way. Each drawer has one bottom, two sides, one back, and one front, so cut these to size. Note that the sides, backs, and fronts need grooves on the inside to accept the drawer bottom.

15 Make the joints between the bottom, sides, and back and assemble.

16 Cut grooves in the sides that will accept the drawer runners. The drawer fronts are applied separately, so make them now and attach them later (see step 25). Make these runners on which the drawers will slide and fit them into the grooves. You can then run the drawers in the cabinet.

The uprights

17 First cut the uprights to size and then make a series of grooves for the side and back panels to sit in. Note that the two rear uprights will need a groove on the two inside faces, while the front two uprights only need one groove each on an inside face. Then drill the ends so that the threaded inserts that will hold the spheres can be fitted. Many hardware stores should sell connectors that have a machine screw thread on one end and a wood screw thread on the other.

18 Now make the wooden spheres for the feet and tops of the frame. The sequence shows these being made in the lathe. First turn the wood into a cylinder and then start to work that into a sphere.

19 When you have achieved this, drill the end of the sphere in the lathe to accept the special threaded insert. Make sure that the thread on this insert is identical on the inserts that went into the ends of the uprights.

20 You should find that these inserts can be screwed into place using an Allen wrench, and you can now assemble the uprights to the base unit using four balls that will become the armoire's feet.

21 To make the top frame, cut the wood to size and make the mitered lap joint. Assemble this frame and, when the glue is dry, trim all around with a plane. Then mark and drill the holes on the corner.

22 Turn this unit over and rout a groove in three sides to accept the side/back panels.

23 Cut the four strips for the pyramid edges and make the central boss, in this case a turned cylinder with a sloping top into which the pyramid edges are joined. Make and fit this joint and fit this component to the frame.

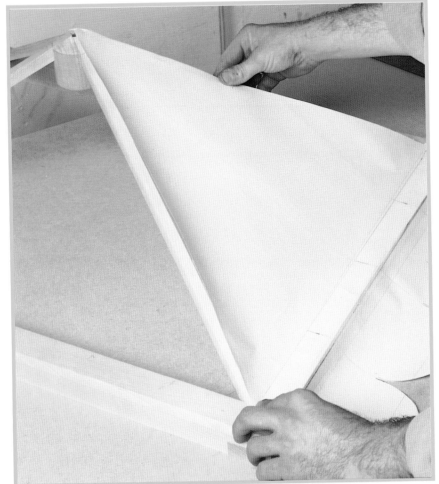

24 This is a good time to make the fabric canopy. Lay out four triangles and scalloped edges in paper and tape these in position over the frame. Transfer the shapes to the fabric and cut out the pieces, remembering to leave ½-inch allowances for seams. Sew the pieces together to make the canopy, leaving a hole at the corners to allow the wooden spheres to be screwed in. Check the hood for fit and remove.

26 Again from scraps, shape two rectangles to make holders for the clothes rod and drill a hole partway through each large enough for the dowel or broomstick. Drill and countersink two screw holes in each holder.

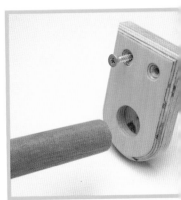

25 Cut three shapes of your choice from scraps of ⅝-inch solid wood for the drawer handles, and three cylindrical pieces to connect them to the drawers. Smooth all pieces to finish, and glue each handle and cylinder assembly to a drawer front. These pieces could be painted before assembly. Then attach the drawer fronts and handles to the drawers themselves.

Assembly

27 Lay out and cut the plywood for the back and sides and fit the back and then the sides, clamping in place, locating in the grooves cut in the uprights.

29 To decorate the sides, lay out your decoration and paint the background yellow. Apply the red for the nose and trousers, then add the blue stripes to the pants. Add the shirt, suspenders, and bowtie, and then the clown's features and hair. Complete the picture with a silly hat and big boots.

30 If you wish, add outlines and details and allow the work to dry. Using a brush or spray, you can now add a clear coat of varnish to seal the work and complete the side. Paint the back in a color of your choice.

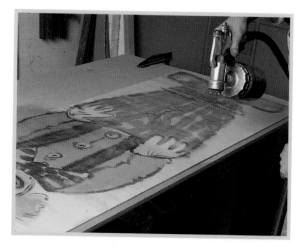

28 You can now assemble the piece. Secure the pyramid to the frame and attach the top frame to the assembly using another four spheres.

31 Now make the curtain closure from the same material used for the canopy. Cut two rectangles of light fabric and turn the edges under. Then cut two narrow dark strips, turn the edges under all around, and sew these on top of the white material. Sew strips of ribbon along the top on the reverse side.

32 Glue and reassemble all the non-glued parts. Screw the two rod holders inside each side, with the dowel or broomstick in place between them. Relocate the side panels in position.

33 Thread the curtain rings onto the wire rod and secure this inside the front uprights in the holes that you have drilled. Then glue or fasten the canopy in place over the frame, place the frame on top of the uprights, and screw the five wooden spheres in place. To finish, tie the ribbons onto the curtain rings to hang the curtains.

Magical Closets

The main theme here was the circus and the easiest way to change the look is by painting different images on the sides. Another approach is altering the drawers and changing them to match the alternative suggestions for the desk and stool set.

Colors and Cutouts

These also work well, especially when a heart theme is used. The unit also looks good in strong, bold colors in stripes as used on the desk and stool set in project 2.

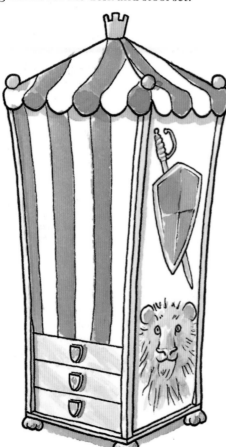

Base Variations

Another effective approach is to change the under-storage to open shelves, a cupboard with hinged doors, or a cupboard with a hinged front.

The Royal This armoire looks excellent with a crown and golden orbs, heraldic devices on the side, lion's feet on the bottom, and more heraldic symbols on the drawer handles.

Index

Credits

Quarto and the author would like to thank all the furniture makers for their contributions and also the parents and guardians of the following children: Timothy Dixon, Jemma and Sophie Heseltine, Samson Jayes, Chloë Keeves and Madeleine Phillips. Props supplied by Pat Byrne, Jo Carlill, Anna French Ltd, London and Susannah Jayes. Thanks also to Maggi McCormick, Kate Robinson, Raye Simpson and Lulu Sturdy.